Printer, typographer, publisher, boxer, sailor, scholar, satirist, wit and poet, Denis Glover was born in Dunedin in 1912 and died in Wellington in 1980. He was educated at Auckland Grammar School and Christ's College, and took an arts degree at Canterbury University College, where he was for some years an assistant lecturer in English and later a College Councillor. He co-founded the Caxton Press in 1936 and published much important New Zealand writing, including the literary periodical *Landfall*.

Glover's own poetry included *The Wind and the Sand* (1945), *Sings Harry and Other Poems* (1951), *Arawhata Bill* (1953), *Since Then* (1957), *Hot Water Sailor* (1962), *To a Particular Woman* (1970), *Diary to a Woman* (1971), *Or Hawk or Basilisk* (1978) and *Towards Banks Peninsula* (1979). He is probably most well known for his distinctively New Zealand poem 'The Magpies', with its 'Quardle oodle ardle wardle doodle' refrain.

During World War II Denis Glover served on loan to the Royal Navy; he rose to the rank of Lieutenant-Commander and was awarded the Distinguished Service Cross for his service in the Normandy invasion. He held an honorary DLitt from Victoria University, a Soviet War Veteran's Medal and, at one time, the New Zealand University welterweight title. For much of his life he lived in Wellington, with a clear view of the sea.

The VUP Classics collection
celebrates more than half a century of stellar publishing
at Victoria University of Wellington

*The End of the Golden Weather* by Bruce Mason *1962*
*Ngā Uruora* by Geoff Park *1995*
*Breakwater* by Kate Duignan *2001*
*Lifted* by Bill Manhire *2005*
*Girls High* by Barbara Anderson *1990*
*Portrait of the Artist's Wife* by Barbara Anderson *1992*
*Wednesday to Come Trilogy* by Renée *1985, 1986, 1991*
*In Fifteen Minutes You Can Say a Lot* by Greville Texidor *1987*
*Eileen Duggan: Selected Poems* edited by Peter Whiteford *1994*
*Denis Glover: Selected Poems* edited by Bill Manhire *1995*

# Denis Glover
# Selected Poems

Edited by Bill Manhire

VICTORIA UNIVERSITY PRESS

VICTORIA UNIVERSITY PRESS
Victoria University of Wellington
PO Box 600 Wellington
vup.victoria.ac.nz

Copyright © The estate of Denis Glover 1995
Editorial matter © Bill Manhire 1995
First published 1995
Reprinted 2019

A catalogue record for this book is available from
the National Library of New Zealand.

ISBN 9781776562831

Printed by Printlink, Wellington

# CONTENTS

Introduction                                          11
Acknowledgements                                      24

### From *Six Easy Ways* 1936

Explanatory                                           27
Home Thoughts                                         28
Sunday Morning                                        29
Epitaph                                               30

### From *Thirteen Poems* 1939

All of These                                          31
The Road Builders                                     32
Holiday Piece                                         33

### From *Recent Poems* 1941

Letter to Country Friends                             34
In Fascist Countries                                  36
Not on Record                                         37
Stage Setting                                         38
The Magpies                                           39
A Woman Shopping                                      40
Thoughts on Cremation                                 41

### From *The Wind and the Sand* 1945

Threnody                                              44
Centennial                                            45
Arrowtown                                             46

Leaving for Overseas                                            47
Sailor's Leave                                                  48
Burial at Sea, off France                                       50

From *Sings Harry and Other Poems* 1951

Sings Harry                                                     51
  Songs                                                         51
  Fool's Song                                                   53
  I Remember                                                    53
  Once the Days                                                 54
  Lake, Mountain, Tree                                          55
  The Casual Man                                                55
  Thistledown                                                   56
  The Park                                                      57
  Mountain Clearing                                             57
  The Flowers of the Sea                                        58
  Themes                                                        59
  On the Headland                                               60
Olaf                                                            61
In Memoriam: H.C. Stimpson                                      62
A Farewell Letter                                               63
For a Child                                                     64
To a Woman                                                      65
Returning from Overseas                                         66
A Note to Lili Kraus                                            67
Off Banks Peninsula                                             68
Dunedin Revisited                                               69

*Arawhata Bill* 1953

The Scene                                                       71
Arawata Bill                                                    72
The Search                                                      73
A Prayer                                                        74

A Question 74
The River Crossing 75
The Bush 76
Incident 76
Camp Site 77
By the Fire 78
His Horse 79
In the Township 79
Living off the Land 81
He Talks to a Friend 81
To the Coast 82
Conversation Piece 84
Soliloquies 85
The Crystallised Waves 87
The Little Sisters 87
The End 88

From *Since Then* 1957

Flame 89
Loki's Daughter's Palace 90
A Sailor's Prayer 91
The Old Jason, the Argonaut 92
The Mother of Christ 93
Polonius' Advice to a Poet 94
Solitary Drinker 96
Towards Banks Peninsula: Mick Stimpson 97

From *Poetry Harbinger* 1958

To a Woman at a Party 101
To a Good Ghost 103

From 'Later Poems', *Enter Without Knocking* 1964

The Little Ships 104

Summer, Pelorus Sound                              106
The Young Sailors                                  108
Evening at the Beach                               109
Off Akaroa – Winter                               110
The Chestnut Tree                                  111

From *Sharp Edge Up* 1968

'No Noise, by Request'                             113
Here is the News                                   115
Electric Love                                      116
The Arraignment of Paris                           117

From *'Even Later Poems', Enter Without Knocking* 1971

Lake Manapouri                                     125
The Vial                                           127
Superstition                                       128

*To a Particular Woman* 1970

Home is the Sailor                                 129
To a Particular Woman                              130
For Myself and a Particular Woman                  131
The Rounded End                                    132
In Needless Doubt                                  133
Brightness                                         134
Island and the Bay                                 135
The Two Trees                                      136
In Absence                                         137
To Her, from Sea                                   138
Two Voices                                         140
The Sea Can Have Me                                141
A Half Farewell                                    142
Before a Winter Journey                            143
Shaping Up                                         144

Afterthought                                    146
Answering a Letter                              147

From *Diary to a Woman* 1971

To a Mermaid                                    148
The Bridge                                      151
Epilogue to a First Diary                       152
About Ourselves                                 153
Sonnet Four                                     154
The Two Flowers                                 155
Down, Puppy, Down                               156
Waiting a Word                                  158

From *Wellington Harbour* 1974

Then and Now                                    159
Impressionist                                   160

From *Dancing to My Tune* 1974

The Pocky Cracked Old Moon                      161
Lovesick for Space                              162
This to Lyn                                     163

From *Come High Water* 1977

What Began it All?                              164
The Author Admonishes the Harbour Sun          165

From *Or Hawk or Basilisk* 1978

John Pascoe                                     166
To a Wife                                       167
A Dead Woman                                    168
The Sick Rose                                   169
A Sailor Finds Love                             170

Printers                                     171
Not for Publication                          173

From *Towards Banks Peninsula* 1979

Bulling the Cask                             174

Uncollected

Pastoral from the Doric                      176

Notes                                        177
Index of Titles and First Lines             186

# INTRODUCTION

When Tom and Elizabeth took the farm
The bracken made their bed,
And *Quardle oodle ardle wardle doodle*
The magpies said.

It's hardly surprising that New Zealand's best-known line of poetry – *Quardle oodle ardle wardle doodle* – should be so determinedly unpoetic. New Zealanders admire doggedness and reticence, and Denis Glover's magpies don't sing: they say. They offer the plain, unmusical facts of the matter. After listening to the refrain a number of times, however, you begin to feel that the magpies are also searching for the conventional harmonies of birdsong – perhaps even for a well-worn verb. Surely this poem is trying to *warble*? Denis Glover's work as a poet, nearly fifty years of it, continually voices a tension between two kinds of articulation: lyric utterance, on the one hand, and on the other the gurgling, gargling sounds of fact and disenchantment. On page after page, he doodles as he warbles – or the other way about.

'The Magpies' is the single New Zealand poem to have achieved a kind of 'classic' status. It interests children as much as adults; and it has a life well beyond the anthology pages – in a range of musical settings, in paintings, and in the theatre. Like the best sacred texts, it also has its own myth of origin. Allen Curnow has recalled (*New Zealand Herald*, 29 July 1987) that Glover composed the poem while driving to visit him at Leithfield, north of Christchurch:

> Glover . . . got out of his little tiny baby Austin in the middle of a wild nor'wester to have a pee by the roadside. There were magpies

squawking everywhere. And when Denis arrived and came to the door of the bach he didn't say anything at all except 'quardle oodle ardle wardle doodle' – just like that.

Indeed, 'The Magpies' is now so familiar that an alternative account of its origin has been confidently offered by the television comedy show *Skitz*. In a sketch written by Dave Armstrong, we are shown the increasingly tipsy poet in the throes of composition, testing and rejecting a range of conventional farmyard noises:

When Tom and Elizabeth took the farm
The bracken made their bed,
And *Arf arf arf arf arf arf*
The sheepdog said.

A number of animals later, he roars: 'Would you magpies shut up! Quardle oodle ardle wardle doodle all bloody day! I'm trying to write a poem here . . .' – at which point a look of slow triumph crosses his face, for indeed a great poem has suddenly found its destined form. The joke has to do with the way in which mundane reality forces itself upon the vision of the inspired poet – which of course simply endorses the poem's point.

It would be wrong to think that Denis Glover's magpies are somehow migrants from a world beyond the poem. More than the inarticulate figures of Tom and Elizabeth, who are known to us only by what they do – or, worse, by what happens to them – the magpies and their stubborn, impure music are essential elements in the poem's own voice. The poem doesn't so much record magpie sounds as utter them; and you can hear magpie noises of one sort or another throughout Glover's poetry. They are there in his sardonic, satirical verses, those constant asides which mock the silliness of the respectable. They are there in his determination to deflate romantic ideals – 'Lili, emotion leaves me quite dismayed,' he wrote, famously, to the pianist Lili Kraus; 'If I'm on fire I call the fire-brigade.' Or you find them in the way his poems, especially in the years before and during the war, borrow the voices of others: Yeats especially, some of the Georgians, thirties poets like Auden and Day Lewis and MacNeice; even the Ezra Pound of *Lustra*.

> My enthusiasm for the tall tree
> and the moon sliding swiftly over the rooves
> knew no restraint.
> Alas there was no-one to tell of it.
> And now you are come at last
> you insist on prattling away about the scenery.

That Poundian observation comes from *Thistledown*, a pamphlet of three poems published in 1935. Its narrative is standard in Glover's work: the enthusiastic declaration no sooner made than displaced. Condemnation of prattling, along with a sneaking regard for it, will be a repeated note over the years. But what seems wrong in this case (and Glover, who was a good judge of his work, never reprinted the poem) is the sense of finality; there is no room left for argument.

*

Denis Glover is never entirely convincing when he aims for absolute statement. A boxer-poet, he is much more impressive when dancing his way through many rounds for a points victory than trying for a single knockout blow. Critics sometimes express disappointment that Glover produced no big poems which seem absolutely central – as if his work was finally no more than a series of interjections made in a world where more sustained and powerful voices were doing all the talking. But very often it is that quality of interjection – of flexibility, of moment by moment responsiveness – which guarantees his poetry's interest. Cumulatively, all the thoughts and afterthoughts and footnotes and asides offer a formal scope and tonal range which make Glover's work far more rewarding than that of tidier poets.

In some ways a 'well-made' poem like 'The Magpies' gives a thoroughly false impression of what he was best at.

The title of another poem, 'Thoughts on Cremation', acknowledges something about Glover's procedures. We are not going to meet a single thought, or a considered conclusion. Rather, what follows will be random jottings, shifting perspectives and registers – nothing too fully *managed*. The poem begins with the formal inversions of ritual lament:

> Not like a fallen feather
> Is he laid away under the high
> Rooflessness of sky . . .

then in section IV a conversational quatrain gets tossed in:

> Would he be done yet, Bill?
> Asked the assistant-stoker.
> – Better give him another minute or two:
> He was a big joker.

while VIII, the final section, which is not quite a conclusion, offers another tone again:

> Have no misgiving
> The man to the mourner said;
> Let us look to the living,
> And earth will look to the dead.

'Thoughts on Cremation' first appeared in *Recent Poems*, the 1941 volume which also introduced 'The Magpies'. (*Recent Poems* was a formidable anthology; as well as a selection of Glover's poems, it included work by Allen Curnow, R.A.K. Mason and A.R.D. Fairburn.) When Glover reprinted the poem in his first major verse collection, *The Wind and the Sand* (1945), he included only sections I, VII and VIII. The poem was reduced to its purely respectable moments. Glover must have decided that, without its variety, without the lowerings into apparent bad taste, his poem had lost an essential part of its character, and he reinstated the full text in *Enter Without Knocking*, the 1964 selected poems.

*

The comic and facetious elements in Glover (which he sometimes herded into separate books with names like *Poetry Harbinger* or *Sharp Edge Up*) are quite as important as the serious and solemn; or, to put it another way, they are part of how he is serious. His versions of reality usually come with their own subversions readily to hand. For a poet who writes with so much formal craft, he can seem astonishingly uneven and casual. Of course, unpredictability is part of the general enterprise – at the end of *The Arraignment of Paris* Glover compares himself to a rugby football in the way he bounces – and by turns he can be serious and flippant, urgent and offhand, sentimental and heartless, inspired and banal. Like some other New Zealand poets – Elizabeth Smither and Hone Tuwhare come to mind – his poetry welcomes incongruity, can seem as pleased with the squib as the skyrocket. In Glover's case this may be related to the anarchic temperament which contemporaries like Charles Brasch thought they glimpsed in him. But it also puts him in the company of poets like William Blake or Stevie Smith, or one or two of Shakespeare's fools.

Thus it makes sense that his poetry should be filled with weather, and with a view of human experience as something primarily composed of the shifting weathers of time and change. In 'Stage Setting', 'the band / Is played by the wind', the sun is a spotlight, and we can see 'in the side-stalls the sea / Moving restlessly':

> And the plot, the plot?
> – How you and I

Were unhutched and crawled
And learned to be.

Then what?
– To grow old, and die.

One notices what will be a persistent interest in age and death. Like James K. Baxter, Glover could use his verse as a way of being old before his time; he had not turned thirty when he wrote 'Stage Setting', was only twenty-three or twenty-four when he wrote the earlier 'Epitaph'.

But 'learned to be' is the interesting phrase in that passage. Within their stage settings – of weather and mountains and sea – Denis Glover's poems are quietly instructive: they show us how we might learn to lead our lives. Their various characters and personae, among whom one counts the love-struck poet himself, are present as simple exemplars of how to exist in the world.

'Learning to be' does not mean evasion or retreat. Sometimes figures like Harry or Arawata Bill are construed merely as recluses and loners, men whose rural existence represents an evasion of the social and political worlds, with all their bustle and hurry. ('Let the world hurry by, / I'll not hurry, / *Sings Harry.*') The natural world may be a simple place, but it too is marked by the processes of time and change; the real evader is the person who settles into a contented complacency which seeks to shut change out. The man who settles for the world of fences – 'And the sea never disturbed / Him fat as a barrel' ('Song') – represents a fairly general failure. As William Blake wrote, 'Do what you will, this life's a fiction / And is made up of Contradiction.' In Glover's work, change and contradiction govern all human affairs. And his most typical poems are those which make change not just part of their subject matter but part of their very behaviour.

The linked, diary-like poems of *To a Particular Woman* are a good example of this. The sequence feels its way forward, coming into being – learning to be – by being true to its word, to the contradictory circumstances and feelings it describes:

> Embrace victory or defeat
> Without pride or rancour,
> Taking what turns up
> Wary of elation, seeking no solution
> That can be predicted or designed . . .
>
> ('For Myself and a Particular Woman')

*To a Particular Woman* charts – and the language is often nautical – the course of a love affair of late middle age (the poet would have been approaching sixty when the events he records took place). The title of the sequence suggests the distinctiveness, the particularity, of the loved one; but it suggests, too, a woman who can be particular in her demands and expectations, whose moments of welcome and reciprocity include a clear sense of what she will and will not put up with. She is desired, but hardly fixed in place – so that the poems addressed to her are full of risk and loss, brief contentments, moments of hope and bafflement and regret, and an occasional cranky elation which is never silly enough to take itself for granted. Glover may have spent much of his time making jokes about love poetry, but he writes about mature love here, with all its twists and turns, to-ings and fro-ings, and tenacious sense of miracle. The opening poem, 'Home is the Sailor', closes with a moment of transformation, where a pebbled shore becomes something more remarkable. Discovery becomes revelation:

> On that sure-traced
> Miraculous psephite shore
> You stood,
> Waiting to be embraced.

There's nothing embarrassed there – or embarrassing. But it is typical of Glover that the conventional conclusion should arrive at the outset: the questing lover has found his loved one in the very first poem. The real love poetry, the true adventuring, will happen hereafter.

*

The voice we hear in *To a Particular Woman* is clearly the poet's own: like Yeats, he is 'walking naked'. But, also like Yeats, many of his more extended enterprises involve the use of a mask – historical figures such as Arawata Bill and Mick Stimpson, or the imagined Harry. These gave the poet ways of expressing obliquely what he felt, without obliging him to answer in person for his feelings or opinions. Perhaps Glover's most obvious mask was donned in 1952 for a single, short poem which gave him an ironic screen for a piece of sermonising. 'Polonius' Advice to a Poet' is exactly what it calls itself – with the implied proviso that Polonius's willingness (in Shakespeare's *Hamlet*) to offer advice didn't do *him* a great deal of good. This Polonius's views on love poetry are often used to gloss Glover's anxieties about the public statement of intimate feelings:

> Love-poems if you like. But keep them short.
> It's all *vieux jeu*, unless you're crude and stark.
> She won't, we needn't, read them. Sport,
> Tell her you love her, and tell her in the dark.

However oblique or direct Glover's phrasings can be, his poems constantly seek out moments of clear perception; the thing they speak of again and again is vision. Vision is exactly where Glover's Polonius begins:

> Upon the unresponsive eye hammer hard words
> Made crystal in clarity,

Leaving feathered thoughts to the birds
And woolliness to handers-out of charity.

If the world's ways of seeing are limited and stale (in *Sings Harry* the eye is 'indifferent', 'accustomed'), the poet's task is to offer another kind of vision. Sight is valuable in itself; but Glover once defined poetry as 'a crystallisation of experience', so insight is important, too. Thus alongside the clear eye of the satirist, there is the weatherwise eye of sailor and climber, the glittering eye of the prospector, the cosmic gaze of the astronomer, the new-kindled eye of the lover, and the mind's-eye of the poet which, fixed in the present, can inspect both past and future by means of memory and imagination. Hence the 'dark-brooding eye' at the end of 'The Chestnut Tree', which sees 'unblinkingly and instantly'. Hence Harry, who sings of what he sees: 'pupil to the horizon's eye', he grows 'wide with vision'; and, in our last glimpse of him, is standing 'hands on hips / [Watching] the departing ships'. In the very last poem in this book, written after he compiled the 1981 *Selected Poems*, Denis Glover mixes his voice with that of a classical shepherd: there he is, above the ocean, his loved one in his arms, contentedly watching his sheep graze.

\*

Polonius also has some words of warning about the poet's material – words:

> Say what you have to say, but beware
> Of nimble-running words that deceive
> Yourself most of all. Words are a snare
> For those who work at a mystery and believe.

Glover speaks as one who has himself occasionally been snared. His love of words is plain throughout his verse – sometimes for better, sometimes for worse. His range of address is rooted in the language he uses: a speaking voice is counterpointed against formal metres, colloquial idioms are mixed with rare and esoteric diction. As Polonius says, it can be a dangerous business: words like 'psephite' may send us in excitement to the dictionary, but too many such will make us close the book. It is hard to know why some phrasings – Gloverisms, they've been called – seem willed and excessive ('Birds nimble the bright air, / Fishes flim in the flood') while others ('The frolic of your dress', 'the inarable, humgruffin sea') seem beyond all argument.

Most of the time Glover had a wonderful ear. Sometimes his liking for risky couplings and hyphenations let him down ('sea-Phoenician-fused'), sometimes alliteration and assonance signal too loudly in the foreground, sometimes his desire to be rid of the superfluous leads to a kind of telegraphese. But his instinct for the half-or slant-rhyme, and for the falling cadence, is always sure. *Sings Harry* has its meanings, but it is the subtle music of the song – the mixed harmonies of certainty and hesitation – that makes us listen:

> To the north are islands like stars
> In the blue water
> And south, in that crystal air,
> The ice-floes grind and mutter
> > *Sings Harry in the wind-break.*

> At one flank old Tasman, the boar,
> Slashes and tears,
> And the other Pacific's sheer
> Mountainous anger devours,
> > *Sings Harry in the wind-break.*

The image of the wave-tusked ocean seems beyond dispute – until you try to imagine it being expressed in the less subtle rhythms of prose.

It's sometimes said that Glover never revised his poetry. Certainly he never followed Yeats and set about revising the workings of his younger self. Yet his moments of vision – their articulation in verse – must have depended crucially on the quiet craft of revision. The notes to this selection record some examples: the way in which *Sings Harry* comes into existence over a ten-year period; the artfulness with which the individual parts of *To a Particular Woman* are arranged. They also trace, loosely enough, how various poems passed in and out of his work whenever he set about compiling a new, retrospective collection. Some, like 'Home Thoughts' or 'Electric Love', changed shape as they came and went. And sometimes you can see the crafty poet giving a half-successful poem the breath of life:

'The rose, the worm, the storm, dark love'
The Commentator now asks what?

Sickly my rose, wriggles the old worm,
And dark, dark is love sunrise or storm
Augmented. (Let the Commentator not
Fall into suburban spinach leaves to rot.)

His leaves are unimportant, his beliefs
Are half-explained half-truths.

But here's your three-in-one,
The god-man-woman toil
Drilling for oil mirthfully
And down to earth.

Press then your plastic nose
To the synthetic rose.
Stay indoor for the storm.
In dark, dark love

A blonde may keep you warm.

'The Sick Rose' appeared in this form in *Landfall* in 1965. It wasn't wanted for the enlarged second edition of *Enter Without Knocking* (1971), but some time after that Glover revised it for inclusion in the 1981 *Selected Poems*. One can see why he did eventually retrieve it, and also why he wanted to make changes – in such a small space the tones of voice clash rather than play against one another; and then, alas, the final line sinks the whole enterprise. (The opposite effect is gained by a similar throwaway ending in 'Loki's Daughter's Palace'.) The revised and rescued poem is printed in the present volume. It is a tighter, tougher piece of work, now pruned to the fourteen lines of a sonnet. At the close of the poem the woman's hair no longer comes out of a bottle; rather than a type – a blonde – she is now a plausibly human figure, one whose warmth may even be real:

Stay indoor for the storm.
In dark, dark love
Her fair hair may keep you warm.

\*

Anthologists are in the happy position of being able to represent Denis Glover at his best. Reduced to a few perfect things – 'The Magpies', one or two poems like 'Threnody', a few pages from *Sings Harry* – his work can hardly be bettered by anything anywhere. But the happy position is not a true one. Glover sometimes wrote about perfection (in 'Printers', for example), but he knew that the human being was a mistake-making animal, and that his own life as a poet was tied up with imperfections. The best parts of *Sings Harry* depend for their lyric grace on their other, less pure moments. And everywhere in Glover's poetry the authenticity of statement is guaranteed by a sort of deliberate, muted awkwardness:

You should have been told
Only in you was the gold . . .

To see Glover clearly, we need more than the anthologist's half-dozen pages. Glover himself was rather too generous to his offspring each time he compiled a selected poems. If you meet too many of his poems in the one place, the interplay of tones and voices begins to repeat, harmonies grow habitual, the unpredictable gets wearyingly familiar. I have set out here to represent Glover's variety and scope, without – I hope – letting the work wear out its welcome. I have used his own *Selected Poems* of 1981 as a starting point. The major sequences are here, uncut; but otherwise I have whittled down the poet's selection. Where sometimes I have added pieces Glover did not favour, there is some indication in the notes; likewise I have noted my one or two departures from the consistently chronological ordering of the *Selected Poems*.

I like every poem in this book, some more than others. I think that 'The Magpies' deserves its fame, and that *Sings Harry* is one of the few astonishing things in our literature. But I am not at all sure that those poems, or any individual titles one might add to them, constitute the *centre* of Denis Glover's achievement. The Glover I enjoy, and admire even more since making this selection, is somehow dispersed through all the parts of his work. On the page he adds up to more than the sum of his parts. His poetry – in all its distinctive moods and formulations – is greater than his poems.

Bill Manhire
Wellington
November 1995

# ACKNOWLEDGEMENTS

My thanks to Rupert Glover, Gordon Ogilvie and James McNeish for encouragement and advice, to friends and colleagues (especially John Davidson) for answering queries and for many conversations, and to the staffs of the Alexander Turnbull Library, Victoria University Library and Wellington Public Library. Thanks, too, to Fergus Barrowman and Rachel Lawson at Victoria University Press. BM

# SELECTED POEMS

# EXPLANATORY

Our reedy fens and hollow logs,
our model pens where wallow hogs,
our very noble native trees,
let others hymn as they may please;

our native birds that lushly sing
pip-toot pip-toot God save the King,
our vines that so obligingly
go crawling up the nearest tree,
are sung by them but not by me;

– or try the guide books. (Goodness knows
our scenery's better than our prose.)

For though the farmer sweats away
to harvest home sweet summer hay
the most of us will find no balm,
no Paradise, no Sabine farm.

# HOME THOUGHTS

I do not dream of Sussex downs
or quaint old England's
quaint old towns –
I think of what may yet be seen
in Johnsonville or Geraldine.

# SUNDAY MORNING

On Sunday the air more naturally breathes,
time stands a little still, and plants put forth
luxurious green life, sweet sunlight weaves
warm patterns on the wall facing the north.

No urgent task, we set our hands upon
hoe, spade or spanner; back-fence gossip tells
epic of artichokes, career of cars; later on
air falls under the heavy yoke of bells.

# EPITAPH

Was born, is dead.
Let this be said
on stone over my head
or graven on urn
when it's my turn.

Sub-edit the stories
or tributes and glories,
nor pausing to dab
slow tear at my slab
sacrifice any flowers
to my leaden hours.

Is anyone stirred
by Whose death has occurred,
or by text like the next?

Let it simply be said
Was born, is dead.

# ALL OF THESE

Consider, praise, remember all of these –

All, blueprint in hand, who slowly rivet
the intricate structure, handle girders like feathers,
take the inert and formless cement, give it
meaning, rearing new walls against weather;

these, guiding surely the sky-swung cargo bales
yawing over black hold; against all gales
they steady with merchandise the rolling mast,
pack tightly the walls of a ship, storm-fast;

these, building together the parts of an engine,
till revolutions, sweetly tension-strung,
instantly answer as control sends in
message to metal, giving lovely tongue;

these whose laboured cunning plough
carves deeply the sweep of the hill's brow;
now with horses clumsily swinging anew
they've creamed over the black earth, arrow-true;

hands, timber-tried, that round the vessel's bow
to take the wave, know prematurely how
the unsalted hull will lift to breaking seas –
consider, praise, remember all of these.

Their easy partnership of hand and eye
divides them not; life they identify
with effortless use of tools, lovely, articulate,
striking clear purpose into the inanimate.

# THE ROAD BUILDERS

Rolling along far roads on holiday wheels
now wonder at their construction, the infinite skill
that balanced the road to the gradient of the hill,
the precision, the planning, the labour it all reveals.

An unremembered legion of labourers did this,
scarring the stubborn clay, fighting the tangled bush,
blasting the adamant, stemming the unbridled rush
of torrent in flood, bridging each dark abyss.

Their tools were pitiful beside the obdurate strength of the land:
crosswire of the theodolite, pick-point, curved shovel,
small tremor of a touched-off charge; but above all
the skill and strength, admirable in patience, of the hand.

These men we should honour above the managers of banks.
They pitted their flesh and their cunning against odds
unimagined by those who turn wordily the first sods.
And on the payroll their labour stands unadorned by thanks.

Who they are, or where, we do not know. Anonymous they die
or drift away; some start the job again; some in a country pub
recount old epic deeds amid that unheeding hubbub,
telling of pitiless hills, wet mountain roads where rusting barrows
    lie.

# HOLIDAY PIECE

Now let my thoughts be like the Arrow, wherein was gold,
and purposeful like the Kawarau, but not so cold.

Let them sweep higher than the hawk ill-omened,
higher than peaks perspective-piled beyond Ben Lomond;
let them be like at evening an Otago sky
where detonated clouds in calm confusion lie.

Let them be smooth and sweet as all those morning lakes,
yet active and leaping, like fish the fisherman takes;
and strong as the dark deep-rooted hills, strong
as twilight hours over Lake Wakatipu are long;

and hardy, like the tenacious mountain tussock,
and spacious, like the Mackenzie plain, not narrow;
and numerous as tourists in Queenstown;
and cheerfully busy, like the gleaning sparrow.

Lastly, that snowfield, visible from Wanaka,
compound their patience – suns only brighten,
and no rains darken, a whiteness nothing could whiten.

# LETTER TO COUNTRY FRIENDS

We in the city live as best we can,
Fettered by fears of by-laws and police.
Our short perspective magnifies alarms;
We feel uneasy when the gas-man calls;
And hopes decline, through tabulated years,
To quarter-acre sections neatly fenced.

Daily across the photographic page
Waddle the imbecile guns; the stock exchange
Is jumpy; over the rented house
Falls the new shadow of a block of flats.

Discarded nightly by a train, and by the gate
Taking the paper from the garden path,
We, in the angle of a clock's hands,
Envy your country lives.

Therefore, beyond the city, we are glad to find
Your country, where the flat roads run
Like helter-skelter hares across the land,
With its frontier the capricious ford
And your fields that lie towards one another,
Mountains being near.

Your ways are ordered, too – though not
By the compelling hours, nor is your dawn
Awakened by the milkman's changing gears.
Your lives are more deliberate: you note
Symptoms in sheep, and gauge the winter feed,
Combat encroaching blight; and all the time
You wage indifferent your war with weather.

Fronting your formidable hills, hedges are toys
And toy-like those scattered buildings;
Nevertheless home to you,
And your wide gates stand open.

# IN FASCIST COUNTRIES

In fascist countries knaves now walk abroad
Meeting with approbation, and the fools
Like headlong rushing stars divert the night.
A thousand prowlers hear the unspoken word

And pry in others' pockets. Letters are opened,
And the traitorous wind, whisking a secret off,
Is ordered to be still. The gates clang to,
And over the prisoner's head magistrates
Serve up cold justice with flamboyant words.

In words dated like medals the junta speaks
Festooned with flowers, and the amplified air
Trumpets each martial and auspicious hour.
The leader-writers like a prodded fire
Burst into flame: truth is a cast-off coat;
And liberty, a cigarette flung down,
Smoulders awhile, and then goes quietly out.

Chart-gazing the astrologers now see
Prodigious portents, and colliding suns
Shatter prediction's glass. Where shall we turn?
Here's a world hurt no herbalist can heal;
And the improbable future what tea-cup will foretell?

# NOT ON RECORD

Ancient and crazed, with eye a-glitter,
The prospector crossed the laborious range
Like a beetle, and was drowned in the bend
Of a river that's not yet named:
Not the gold, but the dream was his end.

# STAGE SETTING

Up-thrust between shoulders of sea
Is the narrow stage, submarine
Outcrop, sea-troubled land-bubble
Ocean top sprouting with green.

This is the scene,
And the curtain goes up
On us all: the band
Is played by the wind.

The sun's the spotlight;
When the play starts
There's no prompter, and no pretence
That the unrehearsed parts make sense.

For audience?
Motionless mountains in the gods
Propping their lids,
And in the side-stalls the sea
Moving restlessly.

And the plot, the plot?
– How you and I
Were unhutched and crawled
And learned to be.

Then what?
– To grow old, and die.

# THE MAGPIES

When Tom and Elizabeth took the farm
The bracken made their bed,
And *Quardle oodle ardle wardle doodle*
The magpies said.

Tom's hand was strong to the plough
Elizabeth's lips were red,
And *Quardle oodle ardle wardle doodle*
The magpies said.

Year in year out they worked
While the pines grew overhead,
And *Quardle oodle ardle wardle doodle*
The magpies said.

But all the beautiful crops soon went
To the mortgage-man instead,
And *Quardle oodle ardle wardle doodle*
The magpies said.

Elizabeth is dead now (it's years ago);
Old Tom went light in the head;
And *Quardle oodle ardle wardle doodle*
The magpies said.

The farm's still there. Mortgage corporations
Couldn't give it away.
And *Quardle oodle ardle wardle doodle*
The magpies say.

# A WOMAN SHOPPING

Beauty goes into the butcher's shop
Where blood taints the air;
The chopper comes down on the block
And she pats her hair.

Death's gallery hangs ready
Naked of hair and hide,
But she has clothes on her body
And a heart inside.

What's death to the lady, pray?
Even shopping's a bore.
– The carcases gently sway
As she goes out the door.

But death goes with her on the way:
In her basket along the street
Rolls heavily against her thigh
The blood-red bud of the meat.

# THOUGHTS ON CREMATION

I
Not like a fallen feather
Is he laid away under the high
Rooflessness of sky
Where the mourners gather
Like leaves blown together:

A room frames this grief;
Falls on the charged air
A loudspeaker's lipless prayer,
And bare walls vouchsafe
A harsher echo of death.

II
Where no sharp outlines print
On tear-blurred eye
Let the obscene lens wink:
The camera cannot cry.

III
The borrowed ritual of the tomb
Has no place in this whitened room:
Though hearts are breaking
Everyone should be smoking.

IV
Would he be done yet, Bill?
Asked the assistant-stoker.
– Better give him another minute or two:
He was a big joker.

V

Please see that I'm cremated,
The busy baker said,
Please see that I'm cremated
When I'm dead.

And on a busy baking day
The busy baker passed away.

Let's put him in the oven,
Was what they said,
Let's make a baker's dozen
With the baker dead.

Although if similarly placed
We might deplore unseemly haste,
We can but praise the thrift that led
To baking him beside the bread.

VI

*That great antiquity, America, lay buried for a thousand years*
                                        Sir Thomas Browne

Consumed by every whimsy of the hour
They've put up crematoria by the score.
When the flower is dead, should we burn the flower?
America, thou should'st be buried as before.

VII

Making their graves in the air,
The Scythians swore by wind and the sword
That the spirit would fly afar
Like a riderless horse, like a bird.

And black on the wave's last slope,
In columned smoke from the cloud
Hung the Viking's funeral ship
Flame-rigged and weapon-proud.

But we have been born of dead
Lying quiet in their graveyard ranks;
They saw it was good to be laid
Under a cross and a word of thanks:

The Christian knows that interment
Is merely a first instalment,
And they sleep well over whom roll
The great cadences of Paul.

VIII
Have no misgiving
The man to the mourner said;
Let us look to the living,
And earth will look to the dead.

# THRENODY

In Plimmerton, in Plimmerton,
The little penguins play,
And one dead albatross was found
At Karehana Bay.

In Plimmerton, in Plimmerton,
The seabirds haunt the cave,
And often in the summertime
The penguins ride the wave.

In Plimmerton, in Plimmerton,
The penguins live, they say,
But one dead albatross they found
At Karehana Bay.

# CENTENNIAL

In the year of centennial splendours
There were fireworks and decorated cars
And pungas drooping from the verandas

– But no one remembered our failures.

The politicians like bubbles from a marsh
Rose to the platform, hanging in every place
Their comfortable platitudes like plush

– Without one word of our failures.

# ARROWTOWN

Gold in the hills, gold in the rocks,
Gold in the river gravel,
Gold as yellow as Chinamen
In the bottom of the shovel.

Gold built the bank its sham facade;
Behind that studded door
Gold dribbled over the counter
Into the cracks of the floor.

Gold pollinated the whole town;
But the golden bees are gone –
Now round a country butcher's shop
The sullen blowflies drone.

Now paved with common clay
Are the roads of Arrowtown;
And the silt of the river is grey
In the golden sun.

# LEAVING FOR OVERSEAS

They make an end at last, binding their friends
With words awkward as names on trees.
Water devours the land, the wave
Mocking every mountain-top of home.

A ship's wake heals slowly, like a wound.

Daily they watch horizons saucer-rim
Slide tilting, where the whale
Takes his gigantic solitary bath. At night
Before the stars' silver tremendous stare
They button up a coat or turn to cards.

Swung on the arc of war towards older islands
Where the thin sun has less to squander
They hold strange course – remembering
And remembering where in the mind's map lie
The road and the mountain,
Islands of home
Pointing a finger at the near north's heart.

# SAILOR'S LEAVE

Oh make me a ballad
About my red red lips
As you cling to them, sailor boy,
My waiting lips.

– All the ballads, all the poems,
Have been written, my dear.
And how could I write any
While you were near?

Then make me a ballad
As if I were not near,
Oh make me a ballad
While you stroke my hair.

– I could make you a ballad
About my drowned mates,
About the clutch of the cold ocean
And the hot deck plates.

But you're on leave, sailor boy,
And life begins again.
– I still remember the tilting deck
And the seas breaking in.

My sweet, my head's on your shoulder,
And your hours are few;
The sea is always waiting
And I've waited, too.

– Then oh lass, my sweet lass,
Pour me out your wine:
The colder kiss of the ocean
Is not yet mine.

# BURIAL AT SEA, OFF FRANCE

Airman, your eager spirit fled,
Too long you rolled in the tide
Unheedingly, unheeded, now not wedded
To those bright wings, now dead.

Taking the sodden papers from your side
What could we do more, with clumsy prayer,
Than give you again to the deep
In which you died?

Burying you we saw the lives that each
In plane, ship, tank or landing craft
Hoped to preserve yet thrust
Numberless, nameless, to the desperate beach,

Necessity compelling. But loss
Even of the ultimate breath
And body of being meant more
Than sad wreckage the waves tossed:

You, airman, from the cloud
Spinning on that last sortie
Played your unwished-for part,
Making our triumph less proud.

# SINGS HARRY

## *Songs*

I
These songs will not stand –
The wind and the sand will smother.

Not I but another
Will make songs worth the bother:
    The rimu or kauri he,
    I'm but the cabbage tree,
      *Sings Harry to an old guitar.*

II
If everywhere in the street
Is the indifferent, the accustomed eye
Nothing can elate,
It's nothing to do with me,
      *Sings Harry in the wind-break.*

To the north are islands like stars
In the blue water
And south, in that crystal air,
The ice-floes grind and mutter,
      *Sings Harry in the wind-break.*

At one flank old Tasman, the boar,
Slashes and tears,
And the other Pacific's sheer
Mountainous anger devours,
      *Sings Harry in the wind-break.*

From the cliff-top a boy
Felt that great motion,
And pupil to the horizon's eye
Grew wide with vision,
> *Sings Harry in the wind-break.*

But grew to own fences barbed
Like the words of a quarrel;
And the sea never disturbed
Him fat as a barrel,
> *Sings Harry in the wind-break.*

*Who once would gather all Pacific*
*In a net wide as his heart*
*Soon is content to watch the traffic*
*Or lake waves breaking short,*
> Sings Harry in the wind-break.

III
When I am old
> *Sings Harry*
Will my thoughts grow cold?
Will I find
> *Sings Harry*

For my sunset mind
Girls on bicycles
Turning into the wind?

Or will my old eyes feast
Upon some private movie of the past?
> *Sings Harry.*

## Fool's Song

All of a beautiful world has gone
– Then heigh ho for a biscuit,
And a buttered scone.
For a dog likes his biscuit
And a man his buttered scone,
    *Sings Harry.*


## I Remember

I remember paddocks opening green
On mountains tussock-brown,
And the rim of fire on the hills,
And the river running down;

And the smoke of the burning scrub,
And my two uncles tall,
And the smell of earth new-ploughed,
And the antlers in the hall,
    *Sings Harry.*

Then Uncle Jim was off to the wars
With a carbine at his saddle
And was killed in the Transvaal
– I forget in just what battle.

And Uncle Simon left the farm
After some wild quarrel,
Rolled his blanket and rode off
Whistling on his sorrel.

My father held to the land
Running good cattle there,
And I grew up like a shaggy steer
And as swift as a hare
While the river ran down.

But that was long ago
When the hawk hovered over the hill
And the deer lifted their heads
And a boy lay still
By the river running down,
  *Sings Harry.*


### Once the Days

Once the days were clear
Like mountains in water,
The mountains were always there
And the mountain water;

And I was a fool leaving
Good land to moulder,
Leaving the fences sagging
And the old man older
To follow my wild thoughts
Away over the hill,
Where there is only the world
And the world's ill,
  *Sings Harry.*

### Lake, Mountain, Tree

Water brimmed against the shore
Oozing among the reeds,
And looking into the lake I saw
Myself and mountains and weeds.

From the crystal uttermost ridge
Dwarfed was the river's course;
Cloud-shouting, to the world's edge
I rode a whole island for my horse.

Forlorn at the last tree,
Grey shingle bruised our bones;
But there holding tenaciously
Were roots among stones.

Knowing less now, and alone,
These things make for me
A gauge to measure the unknown
– Lake, mountain, tree,
    *Sings Harry.*


### The Casual Man

Come, mint me up the golden gorse,
Mine me the yellow clay
– There's no money in my purse
For a rainy day,
    *Sings Harry.*

My father left me his old coat,
Nothing more than that;

And will my head take hurt
In an old hat?
  *Sings Harry.*

They all concern themselves too much
With what a clock shows.
But does the casual man care
How the world goes?
  *Sings Harry.*

A little here, a little there –
Why should a man worry?
Let the world hurry by,
I'll not hurry,
  *Sings Harry.*


### Thistledown

Once I followed horses
And once I followed whores
And marched once with a banner
For some great cause,
  *Sings Harry.*
But that was thistledown planted on the wind.

And once I met a woman
All in her heart's spring,
But I was a headstrong fool
Heedless of everything
  *Sings Harry.*
– I was thistledown planted on the wind.

Mustering is the life:
Freed of fears and hopes
I watch the sheep like a pestilence
Pouring over the slopes,
  *Sings Harry.*
And the past is thistledown planted on the wind.

Dream and doubt and the deed
Dissolve like a cloud
On the hills of time.
Be a man never so proud,
  *Sings Harry.*
He is only thistledown planted on the wind.


## The Park

The river slower moved
And the birds were still.

Leaf and tree in silence hung
Breathless on the plunging sun.

Now came still evening on,
And suddenly the park was full of pedals,
  *Sings Harry.*


## Mountain Clearing

It was a friendly and a private place
  *Sings Harry.*
Where a moss-grown track beside the stream

Led to the clearing in the birches. The face
Of the dark hill above was darkling green.

And in the morning came the sound of the axe
        *Sings Harry.*
Or the bush-buried shot at mountain deer;
The river talked to the stones and
    swamp-smothered flax,
And the hut smoke rose clear.

That was a good place to be camping in
        *Sings Harry.*
Where we unsaddled and hobbled the horses,
Heading over Honeycomb Pass and Mount Thin
For sheep and heat and dust and a hundred water-courses.


### The Flowers of the Sea

Once my strength was an avalanche
    *Now it follows the fold of the hill*
And my love was a flowering branch
    *Now withered and still.*

Once it was all fighting and folly
    *And a girl who followed me;*
Who plucked at me plucked holly,
    *But I pluck the flowers of the sea,*
        Sings Harry,

    *For the tide comes*
    *And the tide goes*
    *And the wind blows.*

## Themes

What shall we sing? sings Harry.

Sing truthful men? Where shall we find
The man who cares to speak his mind:
Truth's out of uniform, sings Harry,
That's her offence
Where lunacy parades as commonsense.

Of lovers then? A sorry myth
To tickle tradesmen's palates with.
Production falls, wise men can prove,
When factory girls dream dreams of love.

Sing of our leaders? Like a pall
Proficiency descends on all
Pontific nobodies who make
Some high pronouncement every week.

Of poets then? How rarely they
Are more than summer shadow-play.
Like canvassers from door to door
The poets go, and gain no ear.

Sing of the fighters? Brave-of-Heart
Soon learns to play the coward's part
And calls it, breaking solemn pacts,
Fair Compromise or Facing Facts.

Where all around us ancient ills
Devour like blackberry the hills
On every product of the time

Let fall a poisoned rain of rhyme,
        *Sings Harry,*
But praise St Francis feeding crumbs
Into the empty mouths of guns.

What shall we sing? sings Harry.

Sing all things sweet or harsh upon
These islands in the Pacific sun,
The mountains whitened endlessly
And the white horses of the winter sea,
        *Sings Harry.*


## On the Headland

Wrapped in the sea's wet shroud
The land is a dream, is a cloud.
The mist and the sun
Have made it their own,
        *Sang Harry,*
And hand on hips
Watched the departing ships.

# OLAF

*(a painting by Leo Bensemann)*

Behind his untamed hair
The sea sleeps like a cat.

The mad blue eye
Sweeps in disdainful stare
Over the mad flat land.

Half lout half dreamer,
Here's one who fought the waves
And thinking murder fun
Would burn a city, colonise a coast,
Urging his sullen oars
Beyond the rim of the world.

Yet lusts for trinkets, violently
After the maelstrom battle
Would wreck his fleet
For some dark foreign girl.

Calling the just unjust,
He's barbarously fair.

# IN MEMORIAM: H.C. STIMPSON

*Port Levy*

You were these hills and the sea,
In calm, or the winter wave and snow.
Lie then peaceful among them,
The hills iron, the quiet tides below.

# A FAREWELL LETTER

Guns mentioned my approach: you did not listen.
And how reluctantly to one
Measuring an exasperated eye
Against the hundredth hazard
You appeared

– You vivid, hostile, planting
Fantastic darts. Lord, it took us time
To clash more potently!

Flashes and fingers of light
Were later lit on us.

Drinking and late and in perversity
Trying to try you, how I failed.
Out at Virginia Water sulking in sunlight,
Longing to love you, drawing some sorry strength
From your cajoling, what a fool I was.

And out of fear of walking naked, hurt,
Engineering with a huge despair
That last fantastic scene.

The story's old. Why should it trouble me
More than the hurts of childhood?
Who saw Cipangu, so they say,
Sickness ate into after.

Well, I'm well.
And if the play is over
One mourns the heroine of course,
But sometime may recover.

# FOR A CHILD

Cave Rock is made of toffee
And the sea of lemonade
And the little waitress wavelets
Are always on parade
   When cars roll down to Sumner
   On a Sunday.

The ice-cream mountain on the blue
Is free for anyone,
And Scarborough Head looms solid
As a tearoom tuppenny bun
   When mum and dad look glum or glad
   At Sumner on a Sunday.

And wistfully the children sit
While Army trombones teach
That only Christ, not Cortes,
Can land upon the beach,
   At Sumner when the seas roll in,
   At Sumner on a Sunday.

# TO A WOMAN

Though the world is torn with care
I am here, and you are here.

We are two, but we are one
When the world leaves us alone;

Nowhere is there less distress
Than in the frolic of your dress;

But nowhere on a pillow is
More than a destroying bliss

And nowhere is there more despair
Than in the tangle of your hair.

# RETURNING FROM OVERSEAS

In the sea's window lie
Island confections on display.

Look, there's Cape Brett, and there
The Hen and Chickens roost on the air.

But to all glad pretence
The land shows indifference.
When we left it sorrow-kissed
Slumbrous, afloat in western mist,
The land of our remembered past
Stood as the loneliest the last
Lovely remote Hesperides
Nourishing its golden trees.

This sullen and perplexing coast
Makes no assertion, no boast,
No positive utterance; and yet
Somewhere there's concealed a threat,
Somewhere home-coming elation
Feels an old strangulation.

Collect the levy book and look
For familiar faces,
Go to reunion dinners
And the races.

# A NOTE TO LILI KRAUS

Walking an unfamiliar road by night
Your playing broke upon me like a light.
Folly and fury and the corroding dream
Were overborne. I voyaged on a stream
Miraculous; and tree and tower and field
On music's Orinoco stood revealed.

Lili, emotion leaves me quite dismayed:
If I'm on fire I call the fire-brigade.
Your music gave me much, I'll say no more,
For like the kiwi I decline to soar.
But in that given and forgiving hour
I breathed the air where the sonatas flower.

# OFF BANKS PENINSULA

Clear and sweet in the crystal weather
The sail and the shroud
Are walking and talking together.

Wind tumbles from the sail, the blocks
Clattering, and the hull dies.

To drift at the cliff's foot
Is to feel the south. The swell
Heaves wide and free like a mature woman,
And the rocks,
Bannered with weed among the gulph
And tumour of the tide
Accept with patience each long kiss.

The far brown hills swelling triumphant
From the plain of blue to the blue sky
Bosom the easy cloud,
Serene and self-possessed rising
Amid illimitable seas endlessly sad.

Wind whispers in: the yacht again
Asserts directions on the trackless tide.

# DUNEDIN REVISITED

A mountain like a beast
Is couched in the north
(Where there is only trouble
And the political bubble).

To the south
Lies a great river's mouth.

Under Flagstaff's boulders
Beds the town; and the houses
Complacent over one anothers' shoulders
Look on a harbour pleasant as a pond

— With gate-crashing rollers just beyond
Where remotely the sugared island still
Winters in the Pacific's hug and maul.

Over the harbour waters
A slow-gonged clock
Floats the hours and the quarters.
From the quarry, all day without shock
Comes the hill-deadened, water-damped
Sound of explosions; and haunting
The frost-quiet of midnight
The redundant the echoing
Bull-breath of shunting.

More eloquent than speech
In probing the dreamlike past
And answering the reproach

By time's soft-fingered shadow cast,
The spires fly heavenward.

A long sunset spills
On those returning,
And the manuka hills
Know the slow smoke of burning.

# ARAWATA BILL

## *The Scene*

Mountains nuzzle mountains
White-bearded rock-fronted
In perpetual drizzle.

Rivers swell and twist
Like a torturer's fist
Where the maidenhair
Falls of the waterfall
Sail through the air.

The mountains send below
Their cold tribute of snow
And the birch makes brown
The rivulets running down.

Rock, air and water meet
Where crags debate
The dividing cloud.

In the dominion of the thorn
The delicate cloud is born,
And golden nuggets bloom
In the womb of the storm.

## Arawata Bill

With his weapon a shovel
To test the river gravel
His heart was as big as his boots
As he headed over the tops
In blue dungarees and a sunset hat.

Wicked country, but there might be
Gold in it for all that,

Under the shoulder of a boulder
Or in the darkened gully,
Fit enough country for
A blanket and a billy
Where nothing stirred
Under the cold eye of the bird.

Some climbers bivvy
Heavy with rope and primus.
But not so
Arawata Bill and the old-timers.

Some people shave in the mountains.
But not so
Arawata Bill who let his whiskers grow.

> *I met a man from the mountains*
> *Who told me that Bill*
> *Left cairns across the ravines*
> *And through the scrub on the hill*
> *– And they're there still.*

*And he found,*
*Together with a kea's feather,*
*A rusting shovel in the ground*
*By a derelict hovel.*

*It had been there long,*
*But the handle was good and strong.*


## The Search

What unknown affinity
Lies between mountain and sea
In country crumpled like an unmade bed
Whose crumbs may be nuggets as big as your head
And it's all snow-sheeted, storm-cloud fed?
    Far behind is the blue Pacific,
    And the Tasman somewhere ahead.

Wet or dry, low or high,
Somewhere in a blanketfold of the land
Lies the golden strand.

    *Mountain spells may bind it,*
    *But the marrow in the bone*
    *The itch in the palm*
    *The Chinaman's talisman*
    *To save from harm,*
    *All tell me I shall find it.*

These mountains never stir
In the still or turbulent air.
Only the stones thaw-loosened

Leap from the precipice
Into shrapnel snow-cushioned.

An egg-timer shingle-fan
Dribbles into the pan
And the river sluices with many voices.

*The best pan is an old pan*
*– The grains cling to the rust,*
*And a few will come from each panning,*
*The rust brown, and golden the dust.*

But where is the amethyst sky and the high
Mountain of pure gold?

## A Prayer

Mother of God, in this brazen sun
Lead me down from the arid heights
Before my strength is done.
Give me the rain
That not long since I cursed in vain.
Lead me to the river, the life-giver.

## A Question

Who felled that tree,
And whose lean-to
Is melting now into that snow?

Barrington or Douglas perhaps
Left these faint tracks

As I, Bill,
Leave my cairns on the hill.

But the mountains on the rim of day
Have nothing to say.
Am I stealing their gold
As a gipsy steals a child,
Am I frisking their petticoats
Camping in the wild?

What do the peaks prepare
For a usurper camping
Where they hold the air
And the river-bend no friend?


### The River Crossing

The river was announcing
An ominous crossing
With the boulders knocking.

'You can do it and make a fight of it,
Always taking the hard way
For the hell and delight of it.

But there comes the day
When you watch the spate of it,
And camp till the moon's down
– Then find the easy way
Across in the dawn,
Waiting till that swollen vein
Of a river subsides again.'

And Bill set up his camp and watched
His young self, river-cold and scratched,
Struggling across, and up the wrong ridge,
And turning back, temper on edge.


## The Bush

Sullen dark bush lies over
The upper reaches,
Thick as a nigger's head
In the coloured pictures
– And no scrub for a bed.

There's nothing yet in my canvas bag
As heavy as this swag.

The door of the valley
Swings shut behind.
But in the next gully
Who knows but I'll find
The colour to make all tongues wag.

Evening hush falls on the bush.
A camp fire on the river stones
Will warm my bones.


## Incident

The constable said one day
'Wata Bill's too long away –
If you're going up by Deadman's Hut
Just look around for a bit.

The route he went,
You'll probably find him stiff
At the foot of a cliff,
Or dead in his tent.

But don't bury him,
Just cover him up.
Leave the body to me –
It's my duty to have the last look.'

When Cashmore saw two legs
Sticking out of a tent
With no camp smoke,
He dragged at them heavy-hearted.
And the sleeper awoke.


## Camp Site

Earth and sky black,
And an old fire's sodden ashes
Were puddled in porridge clay
On that bleak day.
An old coat lay
Like a burst bag, worn
Out in a tussle with thorn.
Water ran
Through a hole in the rusted can.

The pass was wrapped
In a blanket of mist,
And the rain came again,
And the wind whipped.

The climbers had been there camping
Watching the sky
With a weatherwise eye.
And Paradise Pete
Scrabbling a hole in the sleet
When the cloud smote and waters roared
Had scrawled on a piece of board
RIVERS TOO DEEP.

*Wata Bill stuck his shovel there*
*And hung his hat on the handle,*
*Cutting scrub for a shelter,*
*Lighting wet wood with a candle.*


### By the Fire

By the fire he thought of the days
When he was young
And let the world go hang –
At the age of twelve
Running away to the bush.

At the homestead that night a hush
When the lanterned men went out.

They found a fire by a cave,
And two young bushrangers brave
Discussing plans to dispatch
The guard and capture the coach
With a Halt, and a fusilade,
And maybe a bit of a cattle-rustling
On the side.

But they haled them back to work
And the bright dream died.

Dreams don't pay:
There's no gold the easy way.

The embers faded to grey
And the fire was dead
And the moon clanged down
On the metal mountains ahead.


## His Horse

Over forty years of my life
In a kingdom where wind is wife
And all my discourse
Addressed to this old pack-horse,
So strong in patience, so clever,
So wise in the ways of the river.


## In the Township

Said Lizzie the big blonde barmaid, 'There,'
She said to the man at the bar,
'There he is still – it's old
Arawata Bill off looking for gold.'

  *With grub in his saddlebag*
  *And baccy in his pouch*
  *Arawata Bill headed for the Woodhen gulch.*

'He's half-crazed y'know,
Always on the go
– But the only gold he'll ever pan
Is the glitter in his eyes
If you know what I mean.'

*Where is the river flat*
*Where colour shows in the shovel*
*And nuggets as big as berries are found*
*Burgeoning in the gravel?*

'– Comes in with an ounce or two
Sometimes, and goes on the spree,
But there's no talking to the man
He's that far away,

Except with one or two in,
When he'll sing and he'll holler
As good as the best,
Dancing to the victrola.'

*Now I've never tried*
*From the head of the Arawata*
*To the divide and down*
*To the Dart on the other side.*

'Next day he'd go, whether it
Rained or froze.
You'd almost believe
There was something in those
God-forsaken hills he couldn't leave.

Yes, he's a queer one
And not what you might call

Sociable-like – and truth to tell
I expect there's a woman behind it all.'

*Arawata Bill led his horse up the slow hill*
*And his shovel was lashed to his pack.*


## Living off the Land

Catch your kea. That's easy,
Waving a rag on the end of a stick,
Stew him for three hours, and
It's as good a meal as you'll get.

You can always trap eels
In a flax basket
Or shoot duck or fish,
And fill out meals
With good ship's biscuit.


## He Talks to a Friend

Hot springs I've found
Over the other side,
And in the Red Hills
A lode of pure iron
Three feet wide.

Rubies and garnets
In odd patches,
And in one place shale oil
You can light with a box of matches.

The gold? Oh yes, I've got a good clue,
But you'd hardly expect
Me to tell you.


## To the Coast

I
There's no horse this time,
Going's too rough.
It's a man with an eighty-pound pack,
And that's more than enough.

> *Always the colour, in quartz or the river,*
> *Never the nuggets as large as a liver.*

Five years ago I tried this route
Taking the left branch. Now try the right.
It'll mean tramping half the night
Before the weather breaks, turning
Tarns into lakes.

> *The colour is elusive, like streaks*
> *Of wind-cloud. Gold dust must*
> *Come from somewhere. But where?*

Neither river nor mountain speaks.

II
The divide should make a decision here,
Parting the melting trickle of snow
As a woman parts her hair.

And finding a way through this muddle
Of snow and rock on the saddle

My intention is to crawl
Down the far side's precipitous wall
To more of the colour.

> *What metal lies*
> *Between those granite thighs,*
> *What parturition of earth*
> *Yields the golden miraculous birth?*

> *Bee carries golden pollen*
> *Mountain and mist breed schist,*
> *And the swollen river runs sullen*
> *With the dust I have missed.*

III
Jacksons Bay on the Tasman, the end
Of many a search round many a bend.

Does the terminus of the sea
Contain my mystery,
Throwing back on the beach
Grains of gold
I have followed from sea to sea
Thirty times and again
Since I was thirty years old?

> *A seaboot full of gold, tempest tossed,*
> *They hid somewhere on the coast*
> *When their ship was lost.*

But back to the mountains!
I know
The fire of gold
Lies under that cold snow.

## Conversation Piece

*Where are you off to, Bill?*
*Surely the river's too full.*

Me and my billy don't worry:
We take the track for the sea,
And there's no hurry.

*But why are you leaving, Bill,*
*When you've just fetched up?*
*Stay for a bite and a sup*
*Or a few square meals.*

I've tea and sugar and flour,
And inside the hour
I'm heading into the hills.

*Bill, have you struck it rich?*

No – but you never saw such
Promise of colour, not a doubt
Of it – till the cloudburst
Drove me out of it.

*Bill, what will you do*
*When you strike it?*

Me? I might go to town
– I don't like it –
But I'd cut a bit of a dash,
Buy a billycock hat and maybe
Go on the bash.

But I really need
Some tough new boots
And a stout pair of breeks
For crossing the rivers
When the weather breaks.


## Soliloquies

I
The next slip I encounter
May yield the reward
Of the mother lode
Surely by this time owed
By the country I've proved so well.

Who can tell
When the miraculous vein will open
And the golden rain
Cascade into the pan?

II
Curse these mountains, brutes
That send down granite roots
Nourished on the gold
I may never behold.

Someone may find me dead
By the richest lode
With a prize in my hand
That I'm disallowed.

III
When God made this place
He made mountains and fissures
Hostile, vicious, and turned
Away His face.

Did He mean me to burn out my heart
In a forty-year search
In this wilderness
Of snow and black birch,
With only a horse for company
Beating on a white tympany?

Is this some penance
For a sin I never knew,
Or does my Grail
Still lie in the snow or hail?

Yet it might be His purpose to plant
The immaculate metal
Where the stoutest hearts quail.

IV
They'll not laugh this time
When I come home
With something in my poke.
They've been saying too long
That Arawata Bill's just a joke.

The fools. There's more gold beneath
These rivers and mountains
Than in all their clattering teeth.

## The Crystallised Waves

Snow is frozen cloud
Tumbled to the ravine,
The mist and the mountain-top
Lying between.

The cloud turns to snow or mist,
The mist to the stream,
The stream seeks out the ocean
All in a geographer's dream.

What are the mountains on high
But the crystallised waves of the sea,
And what is the white-topped wave
But a mountain that liquidly weaves?

The water belongs to the mountain.
Belongs to the deep;
The mountain beneath the water
Suckles oceans in sleep.

*How are the tops in the dawn?*


## The Little Sisters

The Little Sisters of the Poor
Take me in without demur.
Good meals and a clean bed
And a pillow to my head.
Do they, curing my body's ills,
Know I must go back to the hills?

It sets me dreaming
To watch their gowns as black as birch
And their white wimples gleaming.


## *The End*

It got you at last, Bill,
The razor-edge that cut you down
Not in the gullies, nor on the pass
But in a bed in town.

R.I.P. where no gold lies
But in your own questing soul
Rich in faith and a wild surmise.

You should have been told
Only in you was the gold:
Mountains and rivers paid you no fee,
Mountain melting to the river,
River to the sea.

# FLAME

No one knows the world's end
Nor the end of heart's desire;
And who shall teach the wise men,
Putting folly to the fire?
*Flame burns book and body.*

Once there was a young man
Who rode in a flame:
Dragons dropped withering
Before his fiery name.
*The wise men voted money.*

The young woman married him:
The wise men were relieved
To weigh him down with medals
In which the young man believed.
*Dragons fly through the air.*

Reading long in libraries,
Haunting their halls and schools,
Learning I always learned
Was the prerogative of fools.
*Who can teach a wise man*
*Or work with worked-out tools?*

Wisdom is in the young moon
Climbing in its arc:
The ageing moon is cautious,
Cold, afraid of the dark;
*But light is a sheet of flame.*
*Even flame grows old.*

# LOKI'S DAUGHTER'S PALACE

*Hel, daughter of Loki, goddess of death for all who did not die in battle, dwelt in Helheim. Her palace was Anguish, and her table Famine. She had two waiters, Slowness and Delay, and her threshold was called Precipice. The bed in that place was Care.*

Precipitous the threshold
Of Loki's daughter's palace, sheer
Falling as empty talk down years.

Above the gates of Helheim
ANGUISH it said in clear
Runes carved cold as fear.

The straw-dead comers pressed
Through dark doors gaping wide.
Hel, daughter of Loki, would examine
Each slow approaching guest. Inside

Was rat-squeak music, telling
Only one feasting – Famine.
Shield-like the plates went clattering
In vaulted dark long echoing.

Two waiters, Slowness and Delay,
Dished up cold nothingness
At the drab close of day
Garnished with raftered air.

And so to bed.
And the bed's name was Care.

– Dark lady of that darkened land,
Take my landlady by the hand.

# A SAILOR'S PRAYER

Lord,
Now we're on board
Look after all sailors at sea,
And me.
And remember once more
Our folk ashore.

Keep me out of the Ditch
In the middle watch,
And back from sea
I promise I'll be
At Sunday church
With a clean white front
And polished shoes
And no booze.

# THE OLD JASON, THE ARGONAUT

I sit beside my old ship, the timbers rotting,
Some damned old woman with her entrails telling
How Argo's hull will fall upon my head
For expiation of those expeditious deaths.

What's death? Argo in life was more
Than death's one stroke, as stroke on stroke
Beyond the rubbing-strake
Our oars combed out the water.

Was the Fleece worth it, and the Medea offering
Her warm, cold calculating front?

Yes, but it was, though labours brought
Nothing but glory and the name of Argonaut.

I took her with me on the long haul home.
Trouble and danger there, dark-sleeping
On that sheepskin on the thwart. Dark
Was the homeward voyage, my head at rest
On that dark, treacherously loyal breast.

But she gave me no rest.

Hero-tremendous, and I played the fool.
Vengeful she left me, she
Dragoned in air

– And I sit here, neither alive nor dead,
Waiting beside the Argo and the sea,
An old woman's triumph pouring on my head.

# THE MOTHER OF CHRIST

The Mother of Christ understood
All things of tears and blood
But never knew
What things her Son must do.

Do away with your cant
And your can or your cannot
Understanding a mother's
Not understanding why or why not.

The hurt's in the doing,
Not plain indifference. The hurt
Must be surely as much of His plan
As the best laid schemes of men.

God fails not such
As fail in doing,
Yet from His foreknown ditch
Rise, knowing.

# POLONIUS' ADVICE TO A POET

Upon the unresponsive eye hammer hard words
Made crystal in clarity,
Leaving feathered thoughts to the birds
And woolliness to handers-out of charity.

Be subtle but not too subtle: fools
Crowd always at your elbow and they show
Impudent knowledge of technicians' tools.
Just answer them You Simply do not Know.

Think sometimes of your readers, raiders of thought
Waiting a positive statement, debating
Whether to read you or whether they ought
To take comfort in crosswords or chromium-plating.

Say what you have to say, but beware
Of nimble-running words that deceive
Yourself most of all. Words are a snare
For those who work at a mystery and believe.

Full of fine thoughts, be innocent too.
Be generous to Nature. Poor old dame,
She bears with every poet's point of view
And cooks the seasons' dinners just the same.

Hold to your vision (thinking perhaps of Blake).
You may be brief, you may be Milton-long.
But when they want to tell you that the lake
Is only hydro-electric potential, then they're wrong.

And if they call the Tasman just a puddle,
Something wet in a geographer's dry dream,
Persuade them that their minds are in a muddle,
Disputing hour by hour and ream by ream.

Love-poems if you like. But keep them short.
It's all *vieux jeu*, unless you're crude and stark.
She won't, we needn't, read them. Sport,
Tell her you love her, and tell her in the dark.

Write on (the game's a hard one). Keep on playing.
You may do well, you may decay unread.
Write on, but publish little. – Any delaying
Will leave you old among the dead undead.

# SOLITARY DRINKER

Standing in the same old place
He thought 'I know that silly face.'
And there beneath the spirits shelf
The mirror showed his silly self.

He saw himself with some surprise
A sorry sod with headlamp eyes
AFORE YE GO the slogan read,
But he stayed on and stared ahead.

'I cannot stand this blasted place,
I cannot stand my blasted face.'

The public bar was through the hall:
It had no mirrors on the wall.

# TOWARDS BANKS PENINSULA

### *Mick Stimpson*

I
The water in the long bay
Fingered in and slowly fell away
Hard by your doorstep;

Smooth-sliding the plain of the water
Told you your numbered hours,
Time of netting, time of laughter.
Incorrigible of anecdote, hauling

Out of a deepsea net
Ragtails and rum-soaked rope-ends
Of many a forenoon watch on ships time-dark
(Wave-nuzzling little *Sea Horse*
Or the tallest barque)

You gave the salt its tang
Of Irish oaths, washed rolling down
From a death-green jar.
Your short pipe
Blackened with burning, story ripe,
Would warp the deck beams overhead,
Smelt worse than Jeannie dead
Three days under her own bed.

II
It would take some finding now
Under the coarse hillside grasses,

That place we buried you and meant
To roll a stone to your head,

Planting there the anchor most sailors swallow
Which never again would follow
The curl at the bow of your boat
Round the bays in long summer days.

III
High in those hills your name is forgotten.
But the legend lives on in the yachts
Ghosting to anchorage mud
With warp running out
And the squeal of blocks
And the echoing shout
Of the boats' crews and the boats.

You not there, in that Easter calm
Your face phosphorescent in water
Answers the moon's gleam.

IV
Sure you could mend a net
Better than us with fool fingers
Feeling the crimp and cramp
– Nets knotted and tough like yourself,
Good tarred hemp.

And the fruit your fruit trees bore.
'Spray them be damned.
Have you ever ate
Nectarines like them yet?
I tell ye, salt air is pure.'

'Ye're a liar,' you'd shout.
'Ye set the bluidy net off that point
I told yez t' bluidy well let
Alone to the sharks.
I know by the marks
Of them tears it was sharks.'


V
Beachcomber, Dirty Old Mick,
Was the easiest way to your name,
Proud Henry Charles Stimpson,
Sniggered behind your back
When you'd shouldered your pack
In the pub and hit the track.
Dirty. With your talk of clean ships
And fabulous tonnages
And your plimsoll line higher
Than the pride of bank managers.

And your cocksfooting without booze
While you bought the Maori kids shoes.


VI
Full of sentiment you were. 'May God
Bless our great and glorious Queen Victoria.'
Stiff at attention while a tear trickled,
Old wrinkled warrior.

Deserter too – a Queen's man run
From the lower deck and away
Like a shell from a gun;
And impulsively mad:
Diving into the Bay of Biscay
To rescue an officer's dog.

In a ship if it happened today
They'd stop your grog.

VII
Here from your chosen Port Levy
There was not one bay of the bays
Wouldn't baffle a navy
To fish or to sweep without help:
Every flaw in the weather divined,
Every reef, rock, steep point,
Anchorage, kelp
Bank and current
Engraved on the chart of your mind.

VIII
Now the hills fold over
Your time-elapsed frame.
The cocksfoot and clover
Creepingly cover even your name.

You are salty dust where you lie.
But quickened is the anonymous sea,
And the hours lick endlessly
At the stone of the sky.

# TO A WOMAN AT A PARTY

Behind your silken dress
I sense your silken leg.
But why should I go down
On my knuckled knees and beg?

You'll offer me what you have,
Be it little or much,
But I'm not going to wither up
Before a blowlamp torch.

Tell me what you want of me
And I'll think it over.
But it can only blossom in despair
If you take me for lover.

I've played that old game out,
Riding hell for leather
At fences and ditches. I want
One woman for ever.

Not to be dazzled or bamboozled
Any more by bitches
But to know one woman, leaving
The rest to lechers —

That's my idea. Not new of course
But I wish I'd known earlier
Instead of destroying myself
And getting dried up, and surlier.

So you might as well take
That casual beauty away.
Give me an honest glance and let's
Call it a day.

# TO A GOOD GHOST

Dear ghost, gentle ghost,
Come if you must to haunt this place, this hall.

There's nothing shocking about your presence here
– Your place it was, I'm present host, that's all –

Enter without knocking.

Now there's no longer a familiar face
Do you seek friends not superannuated?
Look in my desk – the same old bills
Older than you but always newly dated
Are mixed with corks and horoscopes and pills.

But here's my unstaged welcome:

You heedless I'm not heartless;
Neither can demons summon
Through art or artlessness;
And utterly I know now and tomorrow,
Only myself can bring on you more sorrow.

# THE LITTLE SHIPS

Matipo, Willomee, Echo
Are the ships in port today:
Ranginui, Titoki, Toa
Plough where dolphins play.

Matipo, Willomee, Echo
May slip on the morning tide;
Ranginui, Titoki, Toa
Berth next at this wharf-side

Where the gulls are quiet
And engines stilled
Holds empty and fuel tanks filled
And sunset clouds run riot.

Headrope and sternfast sway
From bollard to the craft;
Washed, faded dungarees
Are slung to a gantline aft

On Konanda, Taupata, Squall
When these are in. Tuhoe
Will bucket her way through the heads,
Awaiting Holmdale, Kohi.

Harbours and rivers are linked
By the little ships: each knows
Wall of the wharf, wall of the wave,
In turn each comes and goes —

Matipo, Willomee, Echo,
Kohi, Tuhoe, Breeze,
Ranginui, Titoki, Toa,
Patterned to wharves and seas.

# SUMMER, PELORUS SOUND

There is always water.
Every track, half-road or hilltop
Throws a view of the labyrinthine
Seeping and effortless sea
Undulant, insidious, creeping
Round hill and promontory
Unexpectedly.

From the sea, from the boat's deck
Name if you can which lead, which premised peak
Will open up, starboard or port,
The winding road you seek
Of the sea.

There's the beach where powerboats lie,
And brief flashing girls
Swimming and sandalled
Are carefree open to the staring sky
Their boat as idle as a Pharoah's daughter
White-frozen on the varnished water.

Steep-to the anchorage, tree-overhung;
Cook's boats may well have lain here
Anchor up and down; and off this ledge
Blue cod still nose un-traffic-wise
The nibblenook, their eighteen-fathom town.

Watching them, fish for the catching,
Now watch sway
Fathomed warp and delicate weed

Woven and weaving, moving
Upward to the hard skein of day.

Here dawn's a deafening of birds,
End of day a hushed pause, a slow
Curtain drawn over bush and bay.

The sharp splash of oars
Cleaves deep and living water
And dying in defeat the disarmed sun
Leaves, ebbing or flooding,
Water luminous with calm.

# THE YOUNG SAILORS

The wet road of the sea
They followed. Beaconed it beckoned;
They were fancy-free.

Tall-stepped the mast would sway,
The lighthouse looking down
On the boat on the bay.

The fabulous world lay beyond
The sea that angry woman
Wild horse or lipping lover fond.

And furied the wind's fingers
Would tear topping the waves,
The cloud's dark angers

Lightened with laughter
The tiller kicking,
Birds swooping and sailing after.

Time in remembrance sings
Of the shudder and leap of the hull
Planing on shearwater wings.

# EVENING AT THE BEACH

Great heavens! it was stranger far than fiction
And quite miraculous to herself surprised,
For it worked precisely to the prediction
That that good man astronomised –

Venus, the young moon, Jupiter and Saturn
All in conjunction on the same still night!
And just by way of adding to the pattern,
With clockwork regularity, The Brothers' Light.

The sea slept flat, unyawning;
Disconsolately into the darkened west
Clouds drifted off to wait another dawning
Somewhere in Samarkand or Hammerfest.

Dinner was under the veranda awning.

We suddenly sent the sauce bottle soaring
In high parabola, extravagant and foolish.
It shattered against the green gnome's face,
Staining it tomato-red with relish.

# OFF AKAROA – WINTER

Greatly the sea surges
Loud on these ledges
Flailing at looming
Reefs' foam-flecked ridges
Shirted in spray-shift:
Bitter shroud for the boat
That unwarily wanders
In ways dingle-dark.

Sharp-pointed in sorrow
For fishers and folk
Keel-trapped in kelp:
Sharp and hard is that harrow.

Shore-smashing the smother
Dowses mainmast and mizzen:
Unyielding the cliff-front
That seabird rather than
Seaman finds a sure shield.

Whale-waves unravelling run
Ruinous from the world's rim.
Ice-fingered the dim sun.

# THE CHESTNUT TREE

'Hi, old snake!' he said,
Beating the chestnut treasure out of trees,
The lanky cheeky skein of a boy.

But I not yet too old
Looked up to the boy, and the scarlet oaks
And the windmill sycamores in the sky,

And I, who have scotched more snakes
And sloughed more skins
And faced the hydra-headed cobra of the sea,
And the dirty rogue, the suave solicitor,
The dumb power-mounted traffic cop
With his laborious illiterate book,
And poetry lovers and those knowledgeable
About tarts and all the arts,

I thought, 'Me, I'm a damn fool.'
So I watched him up that tree
Beating the unpriced treasure down
Where I saw only a crab-apple past.

And I called, 'Hi, boy! Any big ones?'

He did not reply.
A big one fell as his
Contemptuous libation to the sod.

My body still can weave,
Most lumberingly fast, snake-like in toil,

My tongue whip double-forked
Like vivid-licking lightning
On present and on past.

I moved on past model yachtsmen
Whose model yachts obeyed the model lake.
I thought that that unmodel boy
Tree-hammering and high
Sung out magnificently to me,
And for a moment my dark-brooding eye
Saw unblinkingly and instantly.

# 'NO NOISE, BY REQUEST'

*notice in landlady's hall*

When as a babe I came into the world
  *Holler, burp and bellow*
I made all the noise I jolly well could
Except when asleep on my pillow
And the nursemaid said as they passed the door
'Hush! Silent please or you'll wake the wee chappie
Which means I'll have to change his nappy.'
  *Holler, burp and bellow.*

Mother knitted at my father's friends
  *Karilac diddums doodle*
'If you wake the baby you'll have to go
Back to the Club – you ought to know
If he doesn't sleep he'll never grow!'
  *Click-clack karilac doodle.*

The housemaster waggled away with a cane
  *Bumbo mortarboard jumbo*
'Doesn't it occur to you I can grapple
With the problem of a boy heard munching an apple
And the Head only three pews away in chapel?'
  *Mortarboard bimbo bumbo.*

The foreman yelled from the factory floor
  *Clatter thump and rumble*
'Don't talk to the b. at the other machine
Or you'll lose your hand in the b. guillotine
While the boss is still on the fourteenth green!'
  *Putter, tump and fumble.*

My girlfriend stood outside her door
    *Fidgebottom ho and a hornpipe*
'If you don't go now my Dad will hear,
Him and Mum sleep just in there
– When he wakes up he's as cross as a bear.'
    *Jiggledy Joe and a hornpipe.*

When I was a soldier stiff on parade
    *Eyes-front puggaree chins-up!*
The sergeant suddenly bawled at me
'Keep silence there, you bloody b.!'
When the guns went off I went to tea.
    *Eyes down puggaree wind-up.*

My landlady stood at the top of the stair
    *Bucket of suds and a scrubber*
She said 'Young fella there's too much noise.
Don't gimme that stuff you've been out with the boys,
You're reeking of beer and saveloys,
    *And you're out, you and your cobber.'*

They made no noise at my graveside
    *Mumble shuffle and under*
'Such a well-behaved quiet young man,' they said
(The rain poured down on the parson's head)
'And isn't it awful to think he's dead
    *– And just listen to that thunder.'*

# HERE IS THE NEWS

When the BBC announced
The end of the world,
It was done without haste,
It was neutrally, gentlemanly done,
It was untinged with distaste,
It was almost as if the BBC had won.

# ELECTRIC LOVE

My love is like a dynamo
With woven wire for hair,
And when she brushes it at night
The sparks run crackling there.

Oh she is the magnetic field
In which I pass my days,
And she will always be to me
Electric in her ways.

No insulated force is she:
Galvanic rather, seeing
Hers is the current keeping bright
My filament of being.

Oh yes, my love's a dynamo
Who charges all the air;
My love is an Electrolux
Who sings upon the stair.

# THE ARRAIGNMENT OF PARIS

*(to back-scratchers and rhubarb eaters everywhere)*

Come down, sweet Muse, come down! You mustn't roam
in realms where Gloria finds herself at home,
in realms where Eve with inky footsteps goes
leading the dimpled cloudlets by the nose.
Come down, I say, from where on high there dwell
the solemn saints whom Eileen knows so well –
yield gracefully to all our striving lasses
the grandstand seats on One Tree Hill Parnassus,
nor pause one soulful moment to admire
that Siren-Circe sweet soprano choir.
Unfurl your classic chiton to the breeze,
and parachute to earth with wonted ease
(but not towards our bush so dark and ferny,
for that's been done to death by Mary Gurney).

Come down, old girl, we're going on the spree;
we'll have some fun, before we have our tea;
we'll break a head or two; we'll raise a scandal
before the fifteenth or the sixteenth handle!

* * *

Alas, New Zealand literature distils
an atmosphere of petticoats and frills
(or shall we say, to shock the dear old vicars,
an atmosphere of brassieres and knickers?).
It is a problem for the best of brains,
and yet the melancholy fact remains

that questing for the literary grail
the female is more deadly than the male.

It's but a minor object now to harass
the girls arraigned before our local Paris,
that arbiter of all our arts and letters
presenting rotten apples to his betters.
My proper aim is rousingly to thwack
that self-same Paris on his flinching back
with hearty heaviness – and, if he can,
I hope he'll take what's coming like a man.

A Paris, too, old storied Troy once had:
the pretty boy went early to the bad.
And here's my zeppelin, filled with fireproof helium,
bombing the buildings of a later Ilium.
Stands forth no Hector from those timid fillies?
Wrath is at hand – for here am I, Achilles!

* * *

Paris fares forth today, quitting his lair
where lavender still hangs upon the air;
let's ride a twopenny section on his glory-bus
(carmina quae scribuntur aquae potoribus)
and off we go, behind his willing feet,
to look for Maori ghosts in Manners Street,
or since we have at hand no southern Ardens
to woo his themes in the botanic gardens.

– But who are these, beribboned and befrilled?
Oh can it be the ladies' sewing guild?
But no, they follow Paris – it is clear
these are his sheep, and he their pastor dear.

Our lady poets these: hermaphroditic
he is at once their guide, their friend, their critic.
And with them go a few who by their faces
should be in shoulder-straps instead of braces.
But never mind, they're young – it would be drastic
to make them keep their pants up by elastic.
Let's go with them (but promise to be good!)
and hold platonic picnic in the wood.

See where he leads this little poet band,
trekking ahead to spy the choicest land,
turning a most industrious rural valley
into a sort of Scout and Girl Guide rally.
He sees a farmer (on a mortgaged farm)
and semaphores his sentiments. His arm
beckons the nymphs who more sedately follow,
and in great gulps the scenery they swallow;
out come their notebooks, down go pretty phrases,
up comes the farmer, very blankly gazes,
and then invites them all to get to blazes.

So off they go again, a poet's progress
to seek a fairyland where lives no ogress
sorcerer, wizard or witch – these little Trixies
are more at home among the elves or pixies.
But hark, what sound is that! 'Hark, hark the lark,'
quotes Paris then portentous. What a nark
to find another unpoetic factor:
upon the scene there comes a noisy tractor
and puts them all to rout. Their lark, a sparrow,
comes down to earth and perches on a barrow.

\* \* \*

Paris, good fellow, sponsors all their verse,
rejects the better and accepts the worse
(that line come straight from Socrates, I'll swear!
– If Paris knows his Plato, he'll know where),
a chimney-sweep who'll garner from its cranny
the fireside verse of any rhyming granny,
and when that's done, with industry does he
solicit praise from critics oversea
who tell him solemnly (ye heavens, groan!)
our poetry's as good as England's own.
Tennyson or Browning, also Keats or Shelley,
can be outdone by any high-school Nellie
– you've only got to open wide your mouth
and you'll become a Shakespeare of the South!
You'll beat the English moderns, at the least,
for they've rushed off to hunt the Blatant Beast
of politics or war – the nightingale
they have abandoned to the Daily Mail;
wherefore the critic of the queasy gut
utters a loud admonitory 'Tut!'
and yearns to where (praise be!) Zealandia's daughters
have turned to lemonade great Taupo's waters.

– And Paris now, Maecenas of the story,
sits in an aura of reflected glory.

* * *

Call it half-time, while Paris wipes his eyes:
I've scored a dozen pretty easy tries
and I'm not puffed – so I'll describe my Muse,
a lady some respect and some abuse.

I won't deceive you – she's a shrew (but ah
the nicest sort of women always are).
She leads you on, and then she lets you down,
she gives you all, and then she does you brown.

Mostly as hard as nails, she yet reveals
a most preposterous weakness for ideals.
She loves her friends, yet has confessed
she'd scrap the lot to make a single jest.
But most of all she loves a rousing fight
– in Russia she becomes a Trotskyite,
in Germany she'd want to be a Jew,
among the Irish – well, she's Irish too!

* * *

But back to Paris: we have yet to feature
a lot of facts about this little creature.

People may say, Leave him alone you bully;
he's nothing more than just a little woolly;
he does no harm; he merely reads and writes;
he sinks to no great depths, touches no heights;
leave him alone! To which I'd like to say
Don't interrupt, let's have our bit of play.
He started it, and I'm no compromiser,
he soaped the vent, and I'm the boiling geyser.
– How will he answer back, is what I wonder.
Not in a voice as terrible as thunder,
for Paris likes his literature to be
as well-turned out and manicured as he;
and never does his Muse, a lady pale,
come roaring up the road in search of ale;

oh, she is very much the female gender,
preferring little gems and safe agenda
to great flawed stones, and a poetic splendour.

Or one could say, a herbalist is he
(apply to him: all consultations free)
who'll give you little packages and potions
to regulate the true poetic motions.
Let him prescribe, for any sickness rife;
he'll take away the nasty taste of life.

Above all else, he finds himself fastidious
– he just ignores the things that make life hideous.
He would not serve the Muses as a lackey
where dung lies deep, as in, say, Taranaki.
To coalmine themes he'd never tune his lyre:
he only wants the pictures in the fire.
And lots of little jobs about the farm
he finds are lacking in poetic charm;
for instance, little piggies have to be –
but no, I've got poor Paris up a tree:
to make him sick would make him sick on me
– I'll spare the first procedures that are taken
to turn our little piggies into bacon.

But why should Paris block his dainty ears?
– It's what he's done to literature for years.

* * *

Strangely enough, we've poets in the land
whom Paris doesn't know, or understand.
No Shakespeares these – they'd be the last to boast
that they're in league with even Marlowe's ghost.

But they can leap a five-barred gate of rhyme
and still can keep on whistling all the time,
while Paris and his valiant spinster crew
assault a common stile and then cry 'Phew!'
and cannot mention poetry or art
unless they put a hand upon their heart.

Among them, though, there's one who's fairly good,
a desolated star, a Robin Hood
who ranges round among the greenwood trees
from classic style to rabid journalese,
who turns her pen from sonnet or from ballad
to gossip pars, or recipes for salad.
A pity she should lack a sense of humour;
if she is roused, beware! she's like a puma
this lassie who is never quite the same
without her daily teaspoonful of fame.
But let her be – she's still a giddy gel;
if she keeps on she should do fairly well.

\* \* \*

Paris is last a critic. Turn, my pen,
to criticise this lesser breed of men.

We've far too many critics – all bow-wowsers
who pump up praise from platitudinous bowsers,
inflate flat tyres, wipe windscreens, quickly jump
to pour their oil in anybody's sump.
Our local critics cut most curious capers:
they search for truth, yet work for daily papers.
They're something strange, a kind of currant bun
of journalese and poetry in one.
The magpies and the starlings of the race,

there's nothing that their efforts don't deface.
Eaten alive by advertising vermin
they 'do' an Empire Special, or a sermon,
duly report the Drainage Board's agenda,
and then begin reviewing Yeats or Spender.
It's hard to have to earn your daily bread
by most grotesquely standing on your head,
but Paris is one who does it all for love;
his true reward is waiting up above.
He'll take his place among the angel band,
a volume of BEST POEMS in his hand.

* * *

All right, you trollop Muse, call it a day;
we've had our fun, we've said our little say.
And if the thing's a trifle, quickly done,
they can't object to clean and wholesome fun.
But ah, sweet Paris, how it must have hurt you
to find me making fun of all your virtue.
I've made a hole in your Arcadian thatches
– if you don't like it, here's a box of matches!
Revile my name, in any way you like:
no wicked words can knock me off my bike,
and should you boot me back, let me announce
I'm like a football in the way I bounce.

# LAKE MANAPOURI

For a million years
Or some such improbable time
The lake kept itself to itself,
A policy of isolation.
Bush and mountains generated no myths.

No Lady of the Lake was there to dust
These myriad isles (twenty-nine anyway),
Besom that bosomed floor.

Incurious wildlife saw
In all that water one big birdbath;
Narcissus mountains powdered ballet white
Adored their own deep-frozen forms.

Animated, darling, was your tussock hair
When we lay shoreside naked there.
To my surprise not the lake water bluer
Than your blue eyes, nor drowsy noonday birds
As honey-liquid as your words.

Our Lady Chapel secret cove
Was architraved blue above,
And green green the vestments
Of our invested love,
Love's altar a flat ridge of rock
Indifferent in the sun.

We laughed embraced in loneliness,
Two of us filling that private

Primeval Cathedral with a meaning.
Later returning loved loving
From the dark bush of undrowned bush
We found our altar congregated
With cabinet ministers
As many as it would take
Solemnly and without wonderment of praise
Pissing to raise
The level of the lake.

# THE VIAL

Up in Butler's country I came across it
(Butler the young clever
Kipper chap, not old Hudibras)
In that country oddly misnomered
Mesopotamia, but not oddly now
In present context.

Milky shot glass it was,
Perfect in symmetry, perhaps
Three inches high, among
Those towering peaks
A Rangitata rainbow
In melting hues.

Babylon its birthplace
Five thousand years ago, a vial
Perfect from silicates
First sea-Phoenician-fused.

Babylon treasured it
Then gave it up
From citied middle-rivered lands,

And now homed here
However oddly
To rest in the mist
Of the gorges where
Restless milky rivers meet
In rainbow air.

# SUPERSTITION

Look, I believe in signs, joss-sticks, flares,
Birds flying sinister or right,
A funeral passing, a cross-eyed man,
Spilt salt, a hairpin on the floor,
A horseshoe nailed the wrong way on the door.

Scared-scornful under ladders
I hopscotch pavement squares,
Spit on the dead bird and of course
Cross fingers for a white cat or horse.
On the month's day invoke rabbits or hares.

Portents and omens. Not superstitious I'll
Correct myself with a self-conscious smile.
Knowing each day is my day;
Yet thinking of my dear damned dead
Friends who sailed on a Friday.

# HOME IS THE SAILOR

How did it happen?
The clear course was not
Pre-charted, no favourable wind
Breathed on sails bent
To battle hurricanes,
Bowsed down for bitter spray.
The seas ran sullen
Heavy against the hull.
Lee rocks loomed.

Then there it was,
Suddenly ahead, the haven
Named for you.

On rounding up, sails shivered
Like a wet bird, fell broken-winged.
The warp
Sang out full fathom five
Until belayed.
                      On that sure-traced
Miraculous psephite shore
You stood,
Waiting to be embraced.

# TO A PARTICULAR WOMAN

No more fears.
No more tears
Now, nor over the years.

Avoiding all evasion
Of love or time's erosion,
Oblivious of persuasion

I intend to stay
Endlessly that way
Let come what may.

Trust firms with trust
Found on your breast.
May my metal not rust.

I will be staff and rod,
Answerable to God
In sure mood.

# FOR MYSELF AND A PARTICULAR WOMAN

Why didn't I know before
That to be disarmed
Is greater than to be victor,
That to disarm yourself
Makes yourself conqueror.

Embrace victory or defeat
Without pride or rancour,
Taking what turns up
Wary of elation, seeking no solution
That can be predicted or designed,
Yet facing what must befall knowing,
Flatly, love is all.

Forgive to be forgiven,
Leavening the bread of living.

The past is past; future
Who can knowingly foretell?
The present measures all.

# THE ROUNDED END

Well I can't say anything,
Cast no spell
To untangle your spray-set
Ocean of hair with clumsy fingers,
Nor nibble rabbit-like your hidden ear.

It's all been done before.
I'm thews and tripes and tendons
Just like you. But there is more than that:
Eyes, thighs apart, or any smooth-worn
Sentiments of heart have all been put
Better and before. Don't ask me what
More is in my head. If I knew
It would mean the end of me,
Perhaps of part of you.

Alpha the beginning, Omega the rounded end,
But in between strange letters of love
Spell out variety no man or woman can exhaust
In delight or transient pleasures of the night
Without the mystery of the Spirit and the Host.

Am I frivolously worth you
Even for a while?
The grave and Godlike Christ
Was never known to smile.

# IN NEEDLESS DOUBT

Blow hot the wind, blow cold.
Soon we will both be old,
Wormed with regrets.

Oh let's take
Time's whiskers with a tug,
Light up and let time lag.

# BRIGHTNESS

I am bright with the wonder of you
And the faint perfume of your hair

I am bright with the wonder of you
You being far away or near

I am bright with the wonder of you
Warmed by your eyes' blue fire

I am bright with the wonder of you
And your mind's open store

I am bright with the wonder of you
Despite the dark waiting I endure

I am bright with the wonder of you.

# ISLAND AND THE BAY

The morning light
Creams over Kapiti
Spills on the dark bump
Of Pukerua Bay.

Later, detail will die, then
Island in the clear day
Lie limp, to live again.

Hurrying without hurry
The sun hurries by,
Bypassing island and bay
Where passively they lie.

You lay long passive
Waiting the sun to join
My new-kindled eye
Slowed on the contoured line
Shown in your dawning and day,

You my breasted island, dark bay,
Curved coast of thigh
Now illumined by
Soft lighting of going day.

# THE TWO TREES

In the waste of hours
Two close trees stood and stars
Smothered in daylight
Spoke muffled.

Between two trees
Rainbow delight curved
Up and fell away
To memoried unmoving seas.

Assailing winds howled in
Baffled and attacked again.

The two trees stood

And the rain
Turning to hail and sleet
Lashed at frail
Leaves to draw green blood.

The two trees stood.

# IN ABSENCE

It is intolerable
That you are not here
Head on my pillow
Smelling of your hair.

All will be well. Oh
You will soon be back
Again under my coverlet
To remedy that lack.

Time's piddling rivulet
Is lost in love's great stream
To which I cast myself
Wetly in a bright dream.

# TO HER, FROM SEA

All's lashed and stowed.
We had our farewell kissing.
Black sea is hosing along
The ship's steel flank.

In a fixed smile to every roll
Your photograph sits snug below
Screened in my mind's eye,
Sure certificate to match a certitude
Detached on star-sight, moon's lower limb
Venus escaping on the sky's rim.

To play the sea's salt-bitter game
Is to learn fortitude.
To find again you sorter than
Breathing bulkhead-steel
Is the destined course set
Towards you, purpose
Pitted against the whale-blown
Porpoised sea.

Night has shuttered down.
The far light yammers,
Signalling speed, formation.

I read it without elation
Wetly accept its message thinking only
Of my own renewal
And foreknown destination.
Our answering shutter clatters.

Ship first, then you and me,
All that matters in the face
Of the madly made-up sea

Is love, flesh, mind, salt-tanged,
Three flowers on the mast's steel tree.

# TWO VOICES

*To Her from Me, Waiting*

Looming doomed cliff overshadows
Undermining sea.

Ever-nothing they will outlast
This transience, we
Learning nothing more sure
Than their patience to endure.

*Her, Waiting for Me*

Tree to the cloud
Cloud to the ground.

In ages will be nothing found
Of tree or ground
Or the cloud.

But tree now stands,
And sure ground.

# THE SEA CAN HAVE ME

The sea can have me
At its wish.
A foreknown conclusion
To every merriment,
The expected lash
Salt-bitter against delusion.

I'm not the first
Who plotted on a blank
Chart, sailed a high hope
Until the ship sank.

Sea's cold kills
Old embraces
Obliterating old
Or new faces.

# A HALF FAREWELL

Well that was that.
It was too good
To cradle in a clock's hands
Or outlast time's rough grasp.

We have explored together,
Leaving unmapped
Mountainous countries of mind
And being, such as that other
Hoped we'd never venture.

There was to be more voyaging
More probing of headwaters
Charting of promontories
Thrusting into mouths
Of changing inlets.

The ship's cold copper bottom
Once careened
We'll put to sea again
If you're willing
To face together wind and weather.

# BEFORE A WINTER JOURNEY

The weather weeps. False lashes
Fall away, the withered leaf
Spirals to decay.
Take comfort, love,
The sodden rain will be
Soon cessant, its tears dried
In the avid air of day.
Lie still with me.

The day is not illusion.
Our puzzling highway
Is capriciously signposted
But we know the way.

Lacking no simple faith
Still cradle in my arms, woman,
A frail certainty
Being stronger than stone
Stronger than spiders' webs
Stronger than earth
Or the inarable humgruffin sea
Mouthing toothlessly at milestones
Towards our brighter north.

# SHAPING UP

Woman, you have only once tried
To make me apple-pied
Soft with a threat.

It didn't work.

I'm me yet.

Yet it did work
To make me
Yours yet.

What means what?

You've lost your doubts.
Have I, or not?

No, as you know,
No Eloise and Abelard
No Helen coyed off to Troy with
That no-good Grecian boy
No demotic Gippo telling Antony
Non pro patria,
Poor mumbo-dumbo soldier

Fleshed in joy.
Light feathery feathers
Of the dark
Are different in the daylight's light.

To have and hold the woman
You must fight.

I'm bloodied sure of this.

You encompass me.
There are within the points
Of north and south
Of mind and soul
You and me.

# AFTERTHOUGHT

Everything's right
Love or grief.
Your puzzled educated mind
In some ways ignorant of life
Makes me lovingly laugh.

Not cruelly, but enough.

Finality
I put in chosen banality
Words trivial but true –

I love you.

# ANSWERING A LETTER

You mentioned Poseidon. I know
Too well his vessel-downing
Drowning sailored sea
With more foreboding than I have of you
Or you of me.

That many-changing mesh
I'll set for fish, for flesh,
Overside will pitch
On the crumpet-baited patch
Of shoal ground learned
On which I strand
In patient anger, and anchor.

# TO A MERMAID

I
Your wet and glistening breasts
Rose from the water.

It was so Anadyomene
That I burst into laughter
Glad glorious laughter
With nothing to be said
And much to be thought thereafter.

Emergent you were toplessly alive.

I can swim but I can't dive
So you won't wait till I arrive
To play with you catch-as-catch-can
And grab you by the tail.
My horny hands won't fail.

II
'Tumble me in the tangleweed
Catch my seaweed hair.
Cockles and mussels and pearls
Lie there.

My lips my breasts
Are for the taking, sailor boy.

Jump for them if you dare,
For I destroy.'

III

She sat on her seashore rocks
Combing her golden hair.
Where did she get the comb from?
A wrecked ship maybe,
For it came from the foam of the sea.

Was it a good comb to her golden locks?

Yes indeed. She took no heed,
She looked indifferently
When the ship drove on her rocks.

IV

She loved that sailor boy
And lured him down.
She meant to marry him,
But nothing goes to plan.

V

Snuggle here
And tickle there,
Catch a mermaid by her hair.

But which is what
And where is where
Leaves me submerged
And out of air.

VI

Who says love is stale fish
And beauty but a fisherman's fly
Can go guddle themselves
With that lie. They are wrong.

The current of life runs
Far too strong.

Stem then the salty stream
Fish eye forward;
But be ready to swallow
Your baited dream:
It's you she waits to see
Wriggling her tail
In undulous ecstasy.

She will invite you to lunch.
But in any perplexity
Take no other takers:
Dive downstream
To clean breakers and the gale.

The mermaid's kiss was never real.

VII
Stay soft, love
Never too far from the sea
In which is your life
Your mystery.

VIII
You lapped in fresh water
And suddenly
Your fish tail split
You became all woman,
There was no gainsaying it.

# THE BRIDGE

All the mysteries are dark lights.

God spoke no English
But obligingly sent
Me his latter-day Word
In the flesh.

I accept the Word
Because the Word
Brighter expresses itself
Than a bright sword.

You are the flesh
And for that
I hoist broad pendants to the Lord.

# EPILOGUE TO A FIRST DIARY

Plain words
Conjured up in wonder
Can split mountains and
Icebergs asunder.

# ABOUT OURSELVES

In our separate lives
We unite
Not merely at meal-times
Or in bed in the illuminated night.

Love lives on love and thrives
As it must indeed
On difference. Indifference
Is the prerogative of the dead.

Let's look to the now, looking
Trustingly ahead.
For we are two, yet one,
The moon being complementary
To the sun.

Which precedence has moon, has sun?
The heavens mystery
Is not for mortal woman or for man.

We only know what we have always known,
That without love we live alone.

# SONNET FOUR

Not me. I never knew you were so tough.
That was that. You found the thing untidy,
Me thinking perhaps you were a lady,
A golfing madam, me left in the rough.

Like lots you'd like to take me by the scruff
Of the neck until I cried for mercy
Hollering for Bill, Hone, or Percy
Until you thought I thought I'd had enough.

I fight alone. Watch me, my good woman.
They throw no towel in my canvas ring.

I trust no talisman, need no omen.
Bloodied and beaten, through split lips I sing.

I'm absolutely easy till I die
You in my mind's eye. Let it be that way.

# THE TWO FLOWERS

To man or woman I say
It's foolish to think
It's rose or lilies all the way,
Roses blood-red, lilies that stink.
Take life with both hands,
Take dark blood, take foul,
Then use a towel.

# DOWN, PUPPY, DOWN

I
Yes, I'll be your puppy dog,
I'll be your poodle,
And while you paint
Or etch, I'll scribble.

II
If I loved life
Loving you destroyed me at last,
Not in a drizzle
But in a cloudburst.

III
If need be, while I'm here,
I can hang words
In the invisible air.
I'm not vainglorious of this:
But they by-pass the passing cloud.
I say no more, no less.

IV
You are the reason, woman,
Not the excuse for this loose verse.
It commands itself, commending you
The hot springs of my heart
And my sky rope.
Oh, pass the soap, then towelling
Tell me I'm a dry joke.

V

Don't you dare despise
God's greatest gift, love.
On his behalf I offer that
To my undismayed surprise.

# WAITING A WORD

The moment I give way to despair
Demons gibber through the air.
But laughter breaks in
And I win.

I gravely tell them about you
With passionate dispassion.
They want to make me a 96-gun prize
Broadsided by lies.
I don't tell them you are wonderful
But you are in my eyes
Miraculous in your fashion.

I won't bruise you
Nor shall I lose you:
You are more
Than anything I've had before.

I can be patient like Job
Waiting a word from God.
But by God waiting as I do
I'd sooner have a word from you.

# THEN AND NOW

Yachts walk the weekend water
Loving it anew
As sometimes flat as a pavement
Sometimes deserted as a theatre
Where no ships queue.

Curious water. Over its million years
Still given suddenly to laughter or tears.

Lieutenant Cook, RN,
Was unable to beat in
And Tasman before him,
In the West wind-rove
Had surmised in the South
A gulf or a great river's mouth.

Cook in his breeches from a high hill
Astonished the strait,
Deduced our Harbour,
But the Wind God denied his labour.

The Harbour was canoe-held
Behind the teeth of the reef.

But familiar in disdain
*Hawea*, *Maheno*, now round up.
After a Tasman slogging smooth or rough
Slide alongside at Taranaki wharf
Without benefit of tugging.

# IMPRESSIONIST

Whistler would have painted this
In impressionist anti-Ruskin bliss
Darting his brush in fits
At the unfinished bits, pointing
In self-critical elation
The city lights as a constellation.

Nocturne or Symphony in Grey, he'd say.
Ruffled peacock feathers on water dark
Dark green, drift-clouds miasmal grey.

A ship has just hove in, gale's pawn
Stemming the southerly in the dawn,
And the Harbour not motherly.

Art is greater than Nature,
Said Whistler its great tutor
Sticking out his Thames-fog neck.

Tell that to the sea-booted seaman
Wet on the upper deck.

# THE POCKY CRACKED OLD MOON

The battled earth beats flat
All hopes of lesser man.
They do this, but I do that,
And cruddy my whiskers when
    The pocky cracked old moon
    Goes dancing to my tune.

In a woman is my delight,
Her skirts a Spanish swirl,
Her laughter warm as the night
Drinking from the sun's bowl.
    The pocky cracked old moon
    Goes dancing to my tune.

Birds nimble the bright air,
Fishes flim in the flood,
Trees listen for me for her –
And let it be understood
    The pocky cracked old moon
    Goes dancing to our tune.

We go unbeaten happily
Chancing our lot
Soberly to win victory
Among stars or bones – but
    The pocky cracked old moon
    Goes dancing to our tune.

# LOVESICK FOR SPACE

Ooh, the moony rings of Saturn.
Have I given engagement rings so often?
Must we all honeymoon on Venus
Where no-one's likely to have seen us?

Look to the galaxies, young fool,
Not to the immediacy of the solar sun.
Look beyond girls to the idiot dark

Where there are none none none
But stars delusive bright in space.

Have you ever looked into a moth's eyes,
A moth's light-mad face?

That goes for the stars
And the bloodshot eye of Mars.

# THIS TO LYN

You and I lived others' lives.

But I insist you must live
Your own, stew in your own juice,
Making your own choice.

Be undivided or you're no use.

To be good be selfish.
Turn inward then turn out
Toward the sunflower sun
Who does its day's work
And then folds down.

# WHAT BEGAN IT ALL?

'There is a rock
To guard each sacred harbour,'
Writes a friend, taking stock.

Port Nicholson has several
– They're plug-ugly guards
Posted seaward of Somes and Wards.

What we must wonder is how the sea
Got past so easily.
Over the ages did it lick
Its way in, some stealthy trick
To nibble out soft bays
In timeless devious ways?
Or did the land itself
Jump from the continental shelf
Merely to find
    Bits of itself left behind?
    Yes, that's it. (We've had enough
    Of non-authenticated Maui stuff.)

    The harbour's here. Don't mind it.
    Just take it as you find it.

# THE AUTHOR ADMONISHES THE HARBOUR SUN

After a false start, and cloud-reverses,
The Sun got up to inspect my verses.
He was not impressed, shook a despairing fist,
But crowds of clouds now banner me
And that's how it ought to be.

Said Sun, 'He half-rhymes harbour
With neighbour. Why shouldn't he be
Suppressed, or sentenced to hard labour?'

'Look, Sun, old son,' I made reply,
'I'll sail this cutter full and by.
If you will listen, this is why:
I'll steer for no sun-blistered arbor
Just to get a rhyme for harbour.
Too much full rhyme falls very flat.
(The cat sits on no Harbour Mat.)
Old Sun, you're talking through your hat.'

But verses, verses, what are they?
The wind will blow them all away.

# JOHN PASCOE

*Johnny, Johnny,*
I stumbled many a mile
While you wafted on ahead
With a twitch of a smile.

You whistled in the dawn,
*Johnny, Johnny;*
The keas waddled off in scorn
And I produced a mighty yawn,
*Johnny, Johnny.*

You left me among Rubicon snow,
*Johnny, taciturn Johnny,*
While you poked around for a corncob pipe
You had left there years ago.

You taught me to cross a river,
*Johnny,*
In a way crafty and clear.
But what more can I say of the mountains,
*Johnny,*
What more of the mountaineer?

# TO A WIFE

Look you, necessity of my being,
My mountain, star, and sea –
Your formed woman's mind
Makes things formative for me.

The mountain is a struggle,
The star far away,
And at our door the sea
Licks its whiskers twice in a day.

Stand fast. I don't care tuppence
For whatever happens.

# A DEAD WOMAN

There was a quality there
Always eluding me.
Open in our loving
We closed down other people
Getting in each other's hair
As if they were not there.

You not here, these are sorry words.
Sorry? I apologise for nothing,
Make no pretension to a perfection
Neither of us owned.
Life was our battle-ground.

You were. You were incredible.
Can I say more? Poems to you?
Indirect you taught them
Into the pattern of my thought
Claiming my thought your own, because
Looking back, perhaps it was.

Addressing the dead is a sad poet's trick,
Throwing a last brick.
There's nobody left to replace us both,
Nobody left worth quarrelling with.

# THE SICK ROSE

*(Blake)*

'The rose, the worm, the storm, dark love.'

The curious commentator now asks what?

Sickly my rose, wriggles the old worm,
And dark, dark is love sunrise or storm.

But here's your three in one,
The god-man-woman, toil
In drilling oil for both
Utterly down to earth.

Press then your plastic nose
To the synthetic rose.
Worm, earth, you may refuse.

Stay indoor for the storm.
In dark, dark love
Her fair hair may keep you warm.

# A SAILOR FINDS LOVE

It was an hour of need, Oh
I know now it was meant to be,
But even so – me, I lacked attack
Even in bravado
When I found you crying in your own lack.

Love struck like a torpedo;
As well, shone bright as star-shell will
In black skies. You took me by surprise.

I dried your eyes, and trust shone there
Taking me unaware
Shaming my predatory lies,

And lack of comprehension
Till lip to lip we lost our tension, strange
Magic closing love's loving range
For a direct hit; you, calmer,
Having simplicity and trust as armour.

# PRINTERS

I speak now of printers and bookmen,
Praise men acknowledged great
Whose business has been display of words
Fragile as bones of birds,
Careful of how hyphens mate,
Considering each comma, establishing
A style as precedent for the mile-
Wide errors of authors laughers
At their own inaccuracy.

John Johnson said 'A title page with red
Is affectation. Printing for reading
Or posterity needs only clarity.'
I said to him, 'This book is hand-set, look
And there's no mention of the fact!'
'What affectation could we get to –
And yet, of course, it's affectation not to.'

'Do you like that?' said Oliver Simon.
'Myself I could wish it one-point leaded.'
I who could make no room
On the crowded page of my mind
Had no imperfection to find.

Then Stanley Morison squatted me on the floor
To examine big letter designs and pore
Over the refinement of serifs
With a diffident explanation of why
There was a problem in the kern
Of italic *g* plus *y*.

'That initial's too coarse,' I told Bob.
Lowry said, 'You're a perfectionist, a snob.
I'll get away with it before I'm old,
And to hell with you and Doug Robb.'

'What is perfection?' then I said,
'For type and coffin, both are lead.
Those who sought it did their best
And now find honourable rest,
Dead, dead, dead.'

# NOT FOR PUBLICATION

You know I believe steadfast
In some things; love, one of them.
(For the rest I'll have none of them.)

For years my love-fed trust
Did not corrode or rust,
Giving what I had to give
Not altogether in lust.

Then later again and again
You stole my assured initiative
And led me by the hand
Downed me in your eider promised land.
Later again you cast me forth
With some remorse. I'd like to think
It had been much more than fun for both.
Madly my compass spun
Then settled for magnetic north.

I'll hold my course
In any weather – hail or rain –
Frightened only that you may do
The same deliberate thing again.

# BULLING THE CASK

You told us, Mick,
How to bull a cask,
No easy task
To bull one, no slip,
In a tight-hauled ship.

Ye nimble a bit of light cable
Do ye see, and serves it round
With any old cloth, y' know,
So the chain marks won't show.
Trice it round the round
Bilge-end of the cask
And the cask will behave
At the start of a stave
Lovely rum trickling through.
Mind you, a pannikin beneath.

Unshackle and stow your gear,
Remove the pannikin with stealth.

The stave takes up again
No mark on the belly of the cask.

'Blow me down,' will say Mister Mate,
'It must be this here ewaporation
As has dropped the level of the lake.'

Them days is gone,
The ships, the sailors,
And the rum.

Us then was men, no hanky-panky.
Och, ye've filled me glass.
Skipper, thank 'ee.

# PASTORAL FROM THE DORIC

*Theocritus viii, 53*

Not for me fat far-off lands
Nor guarantee of meat money
Nor even a medal gained
Trimming seconds off the wind.

No. Beneath this rock I sit
You in my arms, fond
Watching my sheep graze,
The rolling blue beyond.

# NOTES

No manuscript or archival material has been consulted for these notes or for the selection. John E. Weir and Barbara A. Lyon's *New Zealand Poetry. A Select Bibliography 1920–1972* (Christchurch, the Library, University of Canterbury, 1977) has been very helpful; it lists magazine and anthology appearances of poems by Glover until December 1972. The following notes contain information on publishing history, textual changes and occasional allusions. They indicate where I have made a choice between different published versions of the same poem; I have made a point of indicating occasions where I have included a poem which Glover did not himself include in his 1981 *Selected Poems*. I hope that in general the notes give some sense of the extent to which Denis Glover *attended* to his work, and to its various arrangements, over many years.

**Home Thoughts.** This poem – which first appeared in *Tomorrow* in 1935, and was collected in *The Wind and the Sand* (1945) – was originally a 24-line poem, and has sometimes been anthologised in that form. Glover omitted it from his 1964 selected poems, *Enter Without Knocking*, reinstated it in the *Selected Poems* of 1981, but kept only a gentle reworking of the poem's last verse, as printed here. The earlier, more confident version of the final couplet read: 'I think of what will yet be seen / In Johnsonville and Geraldine.' Glovers title alludes to Robert Browning's poem, 'Home-Thoughts, from Abroad', which begins, 'Oh, to be in England / Now that April's there.'

**All of These.** First collected in *Thirteen Poems*, 1939, where it was the opening poem. There was an additional final quatrain: 'In the new state all these we will employ: / their lives shall be "endless and singing joy." / They shall build us high towers / against the destroying hours.'

**The Road Builders.** The second poem in *Thirteen Poems*, this became the opening poem of *The Wind and the Sand* (1945).

**Holiday Piece.** In *Thirteen Poems*, the first six lines formed a single, unbroken stanza.

**Letter to Country Friends.** This was the first poem of the Glover selection in *Recent Poems*, a collection of poems by Allen Curnow, R.A.K. Mason, Glover and A.R.D. Fairburn, which Caxton published early in 1941.

**Not on Record.** This became the third poem in *The Wind and the Sand* (1945); it anticipates the 1953 sequence, *Arawata Bill*, in particular 'The End'.

**The Magpies.** The poem's first appearance, already in its familiar form, was in *Recent Poems* (1941). Four years later in *The Wind and the Sand* (1945) the poem has lost its fourth stanza ('But all the beautiful crops . . .'), though this is restored in all other versions of the poem. It seems unlikely that the stanza was omitted by accident. It's *just* possible that Glover the printer sacrificed Glover the poet in order to avoid a turn-over. 'The Magpies' is on p. 29 of *The Wind and the Sand*; the full text of six stanzas would have left four lines stranded at the top of p. 30.

**A Woman Shopping.** First printed in *Recent Poems* (1941); not reprinted in *The Wind and the Sand* (1945), but appears again in *Enter Without Knocking* (1964).

**Thoughts on Cremation.** See the Introduction, pp. 13–14.

**The Wind and the Sand.** Glover's first substantial poetry collection, containing 44 poems in all. The title comes from the opening lines of what is now the *Sings Harry* sequence, which had not yet found its full or final form; the three 'Songs' appear towards the end of the volume under the title 'Sings Harry'.

**Threnody.** The fourth poem in *The Wind and the Sand* (1945), where it was first collected. It had previously appeared in 1935 in the *Canterbury College Review* 87.

**Centennial.** A comment on the 1940 centennial celebrations (the Treaty of Waitangi had been signed in 1840). Unprinted before *The Wind and the Sand* (1945).

**Burial at Sea, off France.** This was the last of the 41 poems collected in *The Wind and the Sand* (1945), and probably the latest in composition. It had appeared first the previous year in the *New Zealand Listener* (November 24, 1944, p. 15).

**Sings Harry.** This group of 14 poems is often selectively anthologised. The whole sequence is printed here, following the text of *Enter Without Knocking* (1964) and the *Selected Poems* of 1981. In fact, *Sings Harry* began as fragments, a range of individual moments, and slowly gathered itself together over a period of about ten years. The opening three 'Songs' first appeared in *Recent Poems* (1941) under the title 'Sings Harry'. 'Fool's Song' was not part of the sequence printed in *Sings Harry and Other Poems* (1951); rather, it faced the Contents page as an epigraph to the whole book. 'I Remember' appeared in *Book* 8 (1946), under the title 'I Remember, Sang Harry'; like the title, its refrain was in the past tense: *'sang Harry'*. 'Once the Days' appeared in *Book* 7 (1946) as 'Harry Singing'. Other individual poems appeared in *Arts in New Zealand, Landfall* and the *New Zealand Listener* between 1945 and 1950. Three poems – 'Thistledown', 'The Park' and 'On the Headland' – were printed for the first time in *Sings Harry and Other Poems* (1951).

**The Park.** 'Now came still evening on.' A direct quotation from John Milton's *Paradise Lost* (Book IV, 1. 598) – a description of twilight in the Garden of Eden, the world of innocence before the Fall.

**Olaf.** The painter and printer Leo Bensemann (1912–86) was a partner in the Caxton Press.

**In Memoriam: H.C. Stimpson.** The poem first appeared in *Arts Yearbook* 6 in 1950. Mick Stimpson was a figure from Glover's youth, associated with the waters around Banks Peninsula. Many anthologies follow early editions of Glover's poems, and use the spelling 'Stimson'. Glover corrected this in *Towards Banks Peninsula* (1979). In that book, 'In Memoriam' is used as an epigraph for the collection as a whole. See the note on 'Bulling the Cask', below.

**For a Child.** Glover alludes again to Cortes (or to Keats's version of him) in 'The End', the concluding poem of the *Arawata Bill* sequence.

**A Note to Lili Kraus.** First published as 'A Note to Lili', *Landfall* 1 (1947), this was the last of a clutch of poems under the general heading, *Poems for Lili Kraus*. Other poems were by James Bertram, Allen Curnow (two) and A.R.D. Fairburn.

Lili Kraus (1905–86) was an internationally acclaimed concert pianist who lived and performed in New Zealand in the years immediately after the Second World War.

***Arawata Bill.*** The sequence was written and published as a separate volume (*Arawata Bill. A Sequence of Poems*) in 1953. What is probably Glover's own note on the dustjacket reads: 'Arawata Bill (William O'Leary) first appeared in the Queenstown district [in] 1898, then aged a little over thirty. He died in 1947. The poems are based on incidents in his life, but in a wider sense they are meant to personify, in Arawata Bill, all the unknown prospectors who essayed rough and wicked country that is not yet fully explored.'

The Arawata River flows down from the Southern Alps in South Westland into the Tasman Sea at Jacksons Bay.

**A Question.** A.J. Barrington and Charles Edward Douglas (better known as Mr Explorer Douglas) were early explorers in the South Westland area.

**The Little Sisters.** William O'Leary was cared for by the Little Sisters of the Poor in Dunedin before his death.

**The End.** 'Rich in faith and a wild surmise.' An allusion to Keats's sonnet 'On First Looking into Chapman's Homer', which proposes the Spanish explorer Cortes's discovery of the Pacific as a metaphor for the inner discovery of a rich realm of the imagination.

**Polonius' Advice to a Poet.** In Shakespeare's *Hamlet*, Polonius gives lengthy advice about manners and morals to his departing son, Laertes.

**Solitary Drinker.** AFORE YE GO. Bells Whisky's advertising slogan: *Bells afore ye go.*

***Poetry Harbinger.*** A joint collection of mostly light and occasional verse from the pens of Glover and A.R.D. Fairburn, ostensibly edited by one Dorothy Cannibal and published by Bob Lowry's Pilgrim Press in 1958. Fairburn and Glover had been planning the volume before the former's death in 1957.

**Towards Banks Peninsula.** In *Towards Banks Peninsula* (1979), this poem is called 'Mick Stimpson II' and is the final piece in the group called *Towards Banks Peninsula: A Sequence.*

'And your cocksfooting without booze.' Refers to the practice of gathering (and selling) the seed of cocksfoot grass.

**To a Good Ghost.** Contains the title of Glover's 1964 selected poems, *Enter Without Knocking.*

**Off Akaroa – Winter.** This poem, which seeks to replicate the alliterative stress patterns and compound nouns or kennings of Anglo-Saxon poetry, was included in *Towards Banks Peninsula* (1979).

**Sharp Edge Up.** Subtitled *Verses and Satires*. An unattributed epigraph contains the title: "'To make fruit juicy before peeling,' said Rinolfo, "you beat it gently with a knife, sharp edge up, so as not to break the skin.'" The author's prefatory note, dated 1967, reads in part:

> These things I would like to think of as a paper monument to idleness, frivolity, bad-tempered nastiness, suppressed roman-ticism, disappointed idealism, youthful optimism, middle-aged pessimism, and an entire absence of rheumatism.
>
> I separated them from my serious verse because I find them rather better. One would hate to be taken for a serious fool.

The contents include the early Caxton booklets *Cold Tongue* (1940), *Summer Flowers* (1946) and *The Arraignment of Paris* (1937), as well as (placed first) many new and uncollected pieces. Few survived into the 1981 *Selected Poems*.

**'No Noise, by Request'.** Karilac. A milk compound for babies.

Puggaree. Term derived from the Hindu word for turban, referring to the thin muslin veil which falls behind a helmet or hat as a sun shade.

**Here is the News.** First printed in the *New Zealand Listener* (August 24, 1962, p. 33). The poet offered a recording of it on *Arawata Bill and Other Verse* (Kiwi SLD–28), released in 1971, but did not include it in the 1981 *Selected Poems*.

**Electric Love.** First published in *Tomorrow* 4 (1938, p. 291). It was part of the group of love poems, *Summer Flowers* (1946), reprinted in *Sharp Edge Up*. Though occasionally anthologised by others, the poem was not reprinted by Glover until the *Selected Poems* of 1981, where he offered the first stanza only, inserting it between poems from *The Wind and the Sand* and *Sings Harry*.

**The Arraignment of Paris.** Not in *Enter Without Knocking* (1964) but included by Glover in his *Selected Poems* of 1981 in its chronological position between work from *Six Easy Ways* and *Thirteen Poems*, i.e. between 'Epitaph' and 'All of These'.

The title refers to the Greek legend in which Paris was charged with the task of judging who was the fairest, Hera, Athena or Aphrodite. He awarded the prize (a golden apple) to Aphrodite, who had promised him the hand of the loveliest woman. This led to him carrying off Helen, wife of Meneleus, which led in turn to the Trojan War. Paris rhymes, conveniently, with the name of the journalist and editor, C.A. Marris, who published an annual magazine, *Best Poems*. Glover saw him as the leader of an unhealthy and outdated literary establishment. 'He was leading New Zealand's poetry along the daisied path of pallid good taste,' he wrote in his autobiography, *Hot Water Sailor* (1962), p. 106, where he also calls *The Arraignment* 'a lovely piece of invective in iambic pentameters' and 'a good rumbustious lampoon'. I have reinstated the asterisks which, in the 1937 booklet, divided the poem into distinct movements.

Gloria, Eve and Eileen, who appear in the first stanza, are the poet Gloria Rawlinson (1918–95), the Australian-born writer Eve Langley (1904–74), who lived in New Zealand between 1932 and 1960, and the poet Eileen Duggan (1894–1972). Mary Gurney was a writer of romantic fiction.

carmina quae scribuntur aquae potoribus. 'Poems written by water-drinkers.' The quotation is from Horace, *Epistles* Book I, 19, 2–3, who refers to the longstanding contrast between the inspired poetry of the wine-drinkers and the lesser, mundane work of water-drinkers.

Maecenas. The literary patron of writers like Virgil, Horace, and Propertius.

Robin Hood, named towards the end of the poem, is Robin Hyde (1906–39). The poem alludes to her first book of poetry, *The Desolate Star* (1929), and to *Journalese* (1934), which was a collection of newspaper and magazine journalism.

**Lake Manapouri.** A poem responding to plans to raise the level of Lake Manapouri for hydro-electric power generation.

**The Vial.** The writer Samuel Butler (1835–1902) spent four years as a sheepfarmer in New Zealand. He called his sheeprun in the Rangitata Valley Mesopotamia. Samuel Butler (1612–80) was the author of the long, mock-heroic poem *Hudibras*.

Kipper. New Zealand naval slang for an Englishman or English sailor.

*To a Particular Woman.* The relationship between this sequence and the poems in *Diary to a Woman* is complex. *To a Particular Woman* (seventeen poems in all) was published in an edition of 300 copies by the Nag's Head Press in 1970; the longer *Diary to a Woman* (66 poems) appeared in an edition of 750 copies from Glover's own Cats-Paw Press in 1971. Each of the 66 poems in *Diary to a Woman* is followed by a date; the work moves in calendar progression from 9 February to 26 November [1970]. *Diary* includes some, but not all, of the poems from *To a Particular Woman*. Where poems are repeated, texts and titles are often different. *To a Particular Woman*, though published earlier, is the more artful selection; poems have been arranged other than in the chronological sequence of *Diary to a Woman* (if the dates in *Diary* are followed, then the poems shared with *To a Particular Woman* were written on 29 April, 22 March, 27 April, 26 July, 7 May, 30 May, 24 June, 17 June, 20 July). In his 1981 *Selected Poems*, wherever there was a choice, Glover preferred the versions of *To a Particular Woman*. The enlarged edition of *Enter Without Knocking* (1971) prints the *To a Particular Woman* sequence in full under its section of 'Even Later Poems', but contains no work from *Diary to a Woman*. The present volume prints all of the poems from *To a Particular Woman*, then a selection of pieces from *Diary*. The poems in both volumes are addressed to the painter and publisher Janet Paul. Glover's 1968 collection, *Sharp Edge Up*, had been published by Blackwood & Janet Paul Limited.

**Home is the Sailor.** In *Diary*, dated 29 April. Small textual differences.

**For Myself and a Particular Woman.** In *Diary*, dated 22 March. No textual variations.

**In Needless Doubt.** In *Diary* as 'Teredo', dated 24 June. The order of the stanzas is reversed. The second stanza is largely rewritten, the first unchanged. Both 'In Needless Doubt' and 'Teredo' appear in *Selected Poems* (1981).

**Brightness.** In *Diary* as 'Avowal', dated 27 April. A few small differences between the two texts.

**Island and the Bay.** In *Diary* as 'The Island and Bay', dated 26 July. Texts differ in some details. The poem was also published in *Landfall* (Vol. 24, 1970, p. 250); text and title as in *To a Particular Woman*.

**The Two Trees.** In *Diary*, dated 7 May. Texts differ in some details.

**In Absence.** Not included in the 1981 *Selected Poems*.

**To Her, from Sea.** In *Diary*, dated 30 May. Small textual differences.

**Two Voices.** In *Diary*, dated 30 May. Some minor textual differences. *Selected Poems* (1981) has no gap between the last two stanzas; *To a Particular Woman* has been followed here.

**The Sea Can Have Me.** In *Diary* as 'Not to Care', dated 24 June. Minor textual differences.

**Before a Winter Journey.** In *Diary* as 'Before an Early Journey', dated 17 June. Considerable differences between the two texts.

**Shaping Up.** Not included in the 1981 *Selected Poems.*

**Answering a Letter.** In *Diary* as 'A Drowned Friend', dated 20 July. Many textual differences. Not included in the 1981 *Selected Poems.*

***Diary to a Woman.*** Dates attached to individual poems are omitted, following the practice of the 1981 *Selected Poems.*

**About Ourselves.** Not included in the 1981 *Selected Poems.*

**Waiting a Word.** The last poem in *Diary to a Woman.* Not included in the 1981 *Selected Poems.*

**The Pocky Cracked Old Moon.** This poem provided the title for the volume in which it was collected.

**This to Lyn.** Not included by Glover in the 1981 *Selected Poems.* It first appeared in the *New Zealand Listener* (October 23, 1972, p. 69) as 'This to a Woman'. Lyn is Gladys Evelyn Cameron (née Stevens), Glover's second wife; they married on 21 September 1971.

**John Pascoe.** First published in the *New Zealand Listener* (March 14, 1969, p. 12) as 'To a Mountaineer'. John Pascoe (1908–72), a well-known mountaineer and writer, was Glover's informant about William O'Leary (Arawata Bill).

**To a Wife.** Not included in the *Selected Poems* of 1981.

**A Dead Woman.** This poem is addressed to Khura Skelton, with whom Glover lived for 20 years, until her death in 1969.

**The Sick Rose.** The first line in quotation marks summarises key elements in the Blake poem of the same name. First printed in *Landfall* (Vol. 19, 1965, p. 17), and considerably revised for the 1981 *Selected Poems.* See Introduction, pp. 20–21.

**Printers.** First published in *Landfall* well over a decade earlier (Vol. 18, 1964, p. 203), and probably prompted in part by the death in 1963 of Glover's friend and fellow printer, Bob Lowry. John Johnson (1882–1956), Oliver Simon (1895–1956) and Stanley Morison (1889–1967) were distinguished printers whom Glover met in the United Kingdom while on war service. John Johnson, the printer at Oxford University

Press, was a particular friend; Glover's letters to him have been edited by D.F. McKenzie ('Poet as / Poet to / Printer: Letters from Denis Glover to John Johnson', in *Sinnlichkeit in Bild und Klang: Festschrift für Paul Hoffman zum 70 Geburtsdag*, ed. Hansgerd Delbrück, Stuttgart 1987). Doug Robb is better known as the distinguished New Zealand surgeon, Sir Douglas Robb (1899–1974).

**Bulling the Cask.** One of the new poems in *Towards Banks Peninsula*, the 1979 volume which brings together older and more recent work based on Mick Stimpson – 'a very real and much-loved man in my Banks Peninsula days,' writes Glover in a note. 'I have tried to reconstruct him in my memory, the substance being fairly true.' In *Hot Water Sailor* (pp. 190–91), Glover records that when he sold his interest in the Caxton Press after the war, he 'thought of making a poetic study of Banks Peninsula, by land as by water. I didn't get around to it – instead I took a job as typographer and typographical adviser to the Pegasus Press.' *Towards Banks Peninsula* is in two parts: *Towards Banks Peninsula: A Sequence*, made up of the Mick Stimpson poems; and *Earlier and Later Pieces on Banks Peninsula*. Like the 1981 *Selected Poems*, the present volume places the early poems ('In Memoriam', 'Towards Banks Peninsula: Mick Stimpson', 'Off Banks Peninsula', 'Off Akaroa – Winter') where they belong chronologically.

**Pastoral from the Doric.** One of two poems submitted by Glover to the literary magazine *Islands* shortly before his death. An editorial note in *Islands* (Vol. 8, no. 3, October 1980) says that 'with the Theocritus translation came the literal parallel (Greek and English) and the note: "Marvellous as English is, the Doric Greek rolls so much better, and has confounded me for forty years."'

# TITLES AND FIRST LINES

Titles are in italics. Initial articles are ignored in the alphabetisation of titles, but not of first lines.

| | |
|---|---|
| A mountain like a beast | 69 |
| *About Ourselves* | 153 |
| After a false start, and cloud-reverses | 165 |
| *Afterthought* | 146 |
| Airman, your eager spirit fled | 50 |
| All of a beautiful world has gone | 53 |
| *All of These* | 31 |
| All the mysteries are dark lights | 151 |
| All's lashed and stowed | 138 |
| Ancient and crazed, with eye a-glitter | 37 |
| *Answering a Letter* | 147 |
| *Arawata Bill* | 71 |
| *Arraignment of Paris, The* | 117 |
| *Arrowtown* | 46 |
| *Author Admonishes the Harbour Sun, The* | 165 |
| Beauty goes into the butcher's shop | 40 |
| *Before a Winter Journey* | 143 |
| Behind his untamed hair | 61 |
| Behind your silken dress | 101 |
| Blow hot the wind, blow cold | 133 |
| *Bridge, The* | 151 |
| *Brightness* | 134 |
| *Bulling the Cask* | 174 |
| *Burial at Sea, off France* | 50 |
| *Bush, The* | 76 |
| *By the Fire* | 78 |
| By the fire he thought of the days | 78 |
| *Camp Site* | 77 |
| *Casual Man, The* | 55 |

Catch your kea. That's easy                                  81
Cave Rock is made of toffee                                  64
*Centennial*                                                 45
*Chestnut Tree, The*                                        111
Clear and sweet in the crystal weather                       68
Come down, sweet Muse, come down! You mustn't roam          117
Come, mint me up the golden gorse                            55
Consider, praise, remember all of these                      31
*Conversation Piece*                                         84
*Crystallised Waves, The*                                    87
*Dead Woman, A*                                             168
Dear ghost, gentle ghost                                    103
*Down, Puppy, Down*                                         156
*Dunedin Revisited*                                          69
Earth and sky black                                          77
*Electric Love*                                             116
*End, The*                                                   88
*Epilogue to a First Diary*                                 152
*Epitaph*                                                    30
*Evening at the Beach*                                      109
Everything's right                                          146
*Explanatory*                                                27
*Farewell Letter, A*                                         63
*Flame*                                                      89
*Flowers of the Sea, The*                                    58
*Fool's Song*                                                53
*For a Child*                                                64
For a million years                                         125
*For Myself and a Particular Woman*                         131
Gold in the hills, gold in the rocks                         46
Great heavens! it was stranger far than fiction            109
Greatly the sea surges                                      110
Guns mentioned my approach: you did not listen              63
*Half Farewell, A*                                          142
*He Talks to a Friend*                                       81
*Here is the News*                                          115
'Hi, old snake!' he said                                    111
*His Horse*                                                   79
*Holiday Piece*                                              33

| | |
|---|---|
| *Home is the Sailor* | 129 |
| *Home Thoughts* | 28 |
| Hot springs I've found | 81 |
| How did it happen? | 129 |
| I am bright with the wonder of you | 134 |
| I do not dream of Sussex downs | 28 |
| *I Remember* | 53 |
| I remember paddocks opening green | 53 |
| I sit beside my old ship, the timbers rotting | 92 |
| I speak now of printers and bookmen | 171 |
| *Impressionist* | 160 |
| *In Absence* | 137 |
| *In Fascist Countries* | 36 |
| In fascist countries knaves now walk abroad | 36 |
| *In Memoriam: H.C. Stimpson* | 62 |
| *In Needless Doubt* | 133 |
| In our separate lives | 153 |
| In Plimmerton, in Plimmerton | 44 |
| In the sea's window lie | 66 |
| *In the Township* | 79 |
| In the waste of hours | 136 |
| In the year of centennial splendours | 45 |
| *Incident* | 76 |
| *Island and the Bay* | 135 |
| It got you at last, Bill | 88 |
| It is intolerable | 137 |
| It was a friendly and a private place | 57 |
| It was an hour of need, Oh | 170 |
| *John Pascoe* | 166 |
| Johnny, Johnny | 166 |
| *Lake Manapouri* | 125 |
| *Lake, Mountain, Tree* | 55 |
| *Leaving for Overseas* | 47 |
| *Letter to Country Friends* | 34 |
| *Little Ships, The* | 104 |
| *Little Sisters, The* | 87 |
| *Living off the Land* | 81 |
| *Loki's Daughter's Palace* | 90 |

Look, I believe in signs, joss-sticks, flares 128
Look you, necessity of my being 167
Lord, / Now we're on board 91
*Lovesick for Space* 162
*Magpies, The* 39
Matipo, Willomee, Echo 104
*Mother of Christ, The* 93
Mother of God, in this brazen sun 74
*Mountain Clearing* 57
Mountains nuzzle mountains 71
My love is like a dynamo 116
No more fears 130
*'No Noise, by Request'* 113
No one knows the world's end 89
Not for me fat far-off lands 176
*Not for Publication* 173
Not like a fallen feather 41
Not me. I never knew you were so tough 154
*Not on Record* 37
*Note to Lili Kraus, A* 67
Now let my thoughts be like the Arrow, wherein was gold 33
*Off Akaroa – Winter* 110
*Off Banks Peninsula* 68
Oh make me a ballad 48
*Olaf* 61
*Old Jason, the Argonaut, The* 92
On Sunday the air more naturally breathes 29
*On the Headland* 60
Once I followed horses 56
Once my strength was an avalanche 58
*Once the Days* 54
Once the days were clear 54
Ooh, the moony rings of Saturn 162
Our reedy fens and hollow logs 27
Over forty years of my life 79
*Park, The* 57
*Pastoral from the Doric* 176
Plain words 152

Pocky Cracked Old Moon, The                              161
Polonius' Advice to a Poet                                94
Prayer, A                                                 74
Precipitous the threshold                                 90
Printers                                                 171
Question, A                                               74
Returning from Overseas                                   66
River Crossing, The                                       75
Road Builders, The                                        32
Rolling along far roads on holiday wheels                 32
Rounded End, The                                         132
Said Lizzie the big blonde barmaid, 'There'               79
Sailor Finds Love, A                                     170
Sailor's Leave                                            48
Sailor's Prayer, A                                        91
Scene, The                                                71
Sea Can Have Me, The                                     141
Search, The                                               73
Shaping Up                                               144
Sick Rose, The                                           169
Sings Harry                                               51
Snow is frozen cloud                                      87
Soliloquies                                               85
Solitary Drinker                                          96
Songs                                                     51
Sonnet Four                                              154
Stage Setting                                             38
Standing in the same old place                            96
Sullen dark bush lies over                                76
Summer, Pelorus Sound                                    106
Sunday Morning                                            29
Superstition                                             128
Themes                                                    59
Then and Now                                             159
The battled earth beats flat                             161
The constable said one day                                76
The Little Sisters of the Poor                            87
The moment I give way to despair                         158

The morning light                                           135
The Mother of Christ understood                              93
The next slip I encounter                                    85
The river slower moved                                       57
The river was announcing                                     75
'The rose, the worm, the storm, dark love'                  169
The sea can have me                                         141
The water in the long bay                                    97
The weather weeps. False lashes                             143
The wet road of the sea                                     108
'There is a rock                                            164
There is always water                                       106
There was a quality there                                   168
There's no horse this time                                   82
These songs will not stand                                   51
They make an end at last, binding their friends              47
*This to Lyn*                                               163
*Thistledown*                                                56
Though the world is torn with care                           65
*Thoughts on Cremation*                                      41
*Threnody*                                                   44
*To a Good Ghost*                                           103
*To a Mermaid*                                              148
*To a Particular Woman*                                     130
*To a Wife*                                                 167
*To a Woman*                                                 65
*To a Woman at a Party*                                     101
To Her from Me, Waiting                                     140
*To Her, from Sea*                                          138
To man or woman I say                                       155
*To the Coast*                                               82
*Towards Banks Peninsula: Mick Stimpson*                     97
*Two Flowers, The*                                          155
*Two Trees, The*                                            136
*Two Voices*                                                140
Up in Butler's country I came across it                     127
Up-thrust between shoulders of sea                           38
Upon the unresponsive eye hammer hard words                  94

*Vial, The*   127
*Waiting a Word*   158
Walking an unfamiliar road by night   67
Was born, is dead   30
Water brimmed against the shore   55
We in the city live as best we can   34
Well I can't say anything   132
Well that was that   142
*What Began it All?*   164
What shall we sing? sings Harry   59
What unknown affinity   73
When as a babe I came into the world   113
When the BBC announced   115
When Tom and Elizabeth took the farm   39
Where are you off to, Bill?   84
Whistler would have painted this   160
Who felled that tree   74
Why didn't I know before   131
With his weapon a shovel   72
*Woman Shopping, A*   40
Woman, you have only once tried   144
Wrapped in the sea's wet shroud   60
Yachts walk the weekend water   159
Yes, I'll be your puppy dog   156
You and I lived others' lives   163
You know I believe steadfast   173
You mentioned Poseidon. I know   147
You told us, Mick   174
You were these hills and the sea   62
*Young Sailors, The*   108
Your wet and glistening breasts   148